TAROT *for* YOU

TAROT for YOU

A WORKBOOK
for Using the Cards to Reflect, Discover, and Grow

Maisy Bristol

ROCKRIDGE
PRESS

First Rockridge Press trade paperback edition 2022

Rockridge Press and the Rockridge Press logo are trademarks or registered trademarks of Callisto Media Inc. and/or its affiliates in the United States and other countries and may not be used without written permission.

For general information on our other products and services, please contact our Customer Care Department within the United States at (866) 744-2665, or outside the United States at (510) 253-0500.

Paperback ISBN: 978-1-68539-739-5 | eBook ISBN: 979-8-88608-980-6

Manufactured in the United States of America

Interior and Cover Designer: Linda Snorina
Art Producer: Cristina Coppin
Editor: Van Van Cleave
Production Editor: Ellina Litmanovich
Production Manager: David Zapanta

All illustrations used under license from Shutterstock.com.
Tarot card Illustrations © Collaborate Agency.

Author photo courtesy of Ariel Rozenbaum

10 9 8 7 6 5 4 3 2 1 0

This book is dedicated to my tarot community. Without you, I wouldn't have had the encouragement or freedom to reach this level of clarity with tarot.

Contents

Introduction

Hi there! My name is Maisy, and I'm so thrilled to see you're ready to dive deep, learn about who you are, and work on yourself with the amazing tool that is tarot. I think many people recognize that tarot is useful, but when they get the cards, they don't necessarily know what to do with them. Many tarot practitioners haven't even scratched the surface of how to use the cards to their full capacity.

That's why this book was created—to show how much tarot can do for us. The tarot journal you are holding is one part experience and one part creativity. In developing this book, I drew on many years of tarot experience to mold personal exercises that I love. But I also expanded my imagination and really pushed the limits of my own beliefs around tarot.

One of my favorite experiences as a tarot reader is seeing that moment when someone has a realization about themselves that they have never consciously considered or put into words. It's part of the reason I'm so certain that tarot is the most helpful tool we have for self-recognition and self-growth.

Here's an example: I once did a reading for a woman who considered herself to be very social—which made her feel confident in large groups. However, the cards I pulled told her that while she is outgoing, this attitude is actually one way she masks her issues of self-worth. Recognizing this allowed her to take steps toward healing. It's experiences like this that really made me recognize how powerful tarot can be.

I've been reading professionally for seven years and practicing tarot for about fifteen years, during which I've experienced my own profound self-recognitions. While I wish I had known about this amazing tool earlier in life, I also believe that we are constantly growing as individuals. There is always work, healing, and processing to do. So, wherever you are in your life, I know this book can help guide you toward self-improvement.

How to Use This Book

This workbook is broken up into various sections that help you focus on the kind of growth you need in that moment. The first part covers the basics of tarot. If you're already a tarot pro, you may still want to skim through it as a refresher and for a new perspective. The second part covers how to use tarot for personal growth, and it divides all exercises into eight different categories:

- Self-knowledge and self-love
- Where you are and where you want to go
- Mental and emotional well-being
- Social life and community
- Love and romance
- Work and prosperity
- Overcoming hardships
- Manifesting joy and resilience

Working with tarot is sometimes referred to as shadow work, meaning a kind of inner work that encourages you to use a psychological lens for self-analysis. It asks you to take a deep dive into many aspects of who you are. How you choose to execute the exercises is up to you, but because of the nature of shadow work, I recommend starting at the beginning of part 2 with the exercises in chapter 3: Self-Knowledge and Self-Love. I believe it's important to start from within and work our way out.

After you feel that you have a foundation, flip through the pages and work on exercises that resonate with you based on your current needs or interests. For example, if you're feeling very lonely right now, you might want to focus on chapter 7: Love and Romance. If you're concerned about your career path at the moment, you might want to start with chapter 8: Work and Prosperity instead.

These exercises are all very simple and easy to understand, and can be done at any time of day. Each exercise will take about ten to thirty minutes, so block out half an hour.

Remember: How you want to take this journey is up to you. It is *your* journey, after all.

PART I

An Introduction to Tarot for Personal Growth

This section of the book will bring you back to the beginning: what tarot is and how it originated. In doing so, we will uncover how tarot was used in the past and how it has evolved over time. Even if you're familiar with tarot, this is a great place to start, as it should reframe your mind and get you into the right headspace to start the exercises. This section covers how tarot works, how it originated, the difference between the Major and Minor Arcana, and the different kinds of decks that are out there.

After the basics, we'll approach how tarot can be used as a personal growth tool. This is the part that is absolutely necessary for you to read. You'll need to understand what makes tarot unique in accessing the human psyche, tapping into your core feelings, and recognizing hidden truths. In general, this section will cover tarot's unique properties as well as how to determine clear intentions and prepare your deck for readings. Once you understand these topics, you will be better equipped to trust tarot to bring messages in your exercises.

CHAPTER 1

REVISITING THE BASICS

When people think about tarot cards, thoughts of psychic party entertainers or dimly lit Los Angeles storefronts often come to mind. Thankfully, this stigmatized view of tarot is becoming less popular. Tarot cards are so much more than a cheap party trick, and modern culture has started to embrace tarot as a self-help practice. With proper understanding and knowledge, a deck of cards can truly help you revolutionize your life.

That's where this journal comes in. In this first section, we'll cover everything you need to know before you start digging into who you are. We will first define what tarot is, then cover everything from its history to how it works. Finally, we will define each of the seventy-eight cards in the tarot deck to help get you started on your self-growth journey.

What Is Tarot?

At their core, tarot cards are a divinatory tool that can offer insight into life changes, personal questions, disoriented thoughts, and self-development. The exercises in this workbook will demonstrate how helpful tarot can be in exploring themes of self-progression and self-exploration.

Tarot only requires you. Unlike other divination methods like astrology—where the practice draws from the information or inclusion of real-time moving planets—tarot answers to you and you alone. Because of that, tarot promotes direct communication with your most authentic and truthful self. It exists as a conduit to help you get closer to the real you.

Additionally, because tarot is a third-party outlet that's also an inanimate object, it offers more freedom to be vulnerable. Using tarot cards offers the benefit of an intimate, closed-door situation where we can be *real* without the pressing worry of being judged. With just "me, myself, and I," we have the opportunity to really transform.

To me, reading tarot cards is like journaling. When you pull a bunch of cards out together and they lay scattered in front of you, they represent the fragmented parts of the mind. The job of the tarot reader is to make sense of the fragments and find a flowing narrative. Whatever you're thinking intuitively or subconsciously is what will appear on the table. This is what makes tarot readings so powerful. Blatantly direct answers from within become inescapable. Plus, it is much more difficult to hide from answers when they come from cards that *you've* picked.

Tarot's Origins and History

The earliest forms of tarot were used solely for entertainment purposes. Egyptian cards displayed the likes of gods and goddesses, Italian cards were used as games and showed everyday situations, and French cards were reserved for nobility and portrayed religious symbols and motifs.

While the origin of tarot is unknown, French occultist Jean-Baptiste Alliette (who wrote under the pseudonym "Etteilla") claimed in 1791 that the Egyptian *Book of Thoth* was the source of inspiration for the first tarot cards.

However, the first recorded appearance of tarot was in sixteenth-century Italy, using the cards for games similar to Hearts (called *tarocchini*) and for a whimsical fortune-telling game called *tarocchi appropriati*. The Visconti-Sforza tarot deck, the oldest deck preserved, was the preferred deck during this time.

The traditional seventy-eight-card format that we use today originated at the start of the eighteenth century with the *Tarot de Marseilles*, published in 1701 in France.

During the nineteenth and early twentieth centuries, tarot's beginnings in Europe collided with the Victorian era's fascination with the paranormal and the occult. Tarot was revered as a divinatory tool, which opened the gate for the most famous deck of all: the Rider-Waite tarot deck. Published in 1910 in England, this is the most popular and widely recognized deck today.

After the turn of the century, tarot's immense popularity fizzled for a while. But recently, tarot and astrology have experienced a resurgence. Today you can find hundreds of different tarot decks with unique themes.

Types of Decks

There are two types of divinatory decks out there: tarot decks and oracle decks.

When you want direct answers, tarot is what you need. When you're looking for inspiration or an uplifting boost, oracle decks are best. Oracle decks tend to have very basic or positive meanings. On the other hand, tarot can result in extremely in-depth readings, often offering multiple meanings for each card.

Additionally, tarot decks are more traditional and structured than oracle decks. Every tarot deck is created with the same intention and the same tried-and-true format. Oracle decks, on the other hand, are all different and don't necessarily take inspiration from the same artwork or symbolism. Also, oracle decks aren't limited to four suits; they could have five or two, or no suits at all.

Tarot decks are wonderful for deep soul-searching and self-progression. (That's why owning a tarot deck is key for this workbook.) Oracle decks are ideal for moments when you need a pick-me-up or are asking for simple advice.

Here is a quick guide covering three of the most famous (and historic) tarot decks out there.

Tarot de Marseilles

This deck catalyzed the seventy-eight-card structure that we use in tarot decks today. Though its name might imply that it is a French deck, it actually originated in Italy during the fifteenth century.

The artwork in the Minor Arcana is very simple, showing just suits. As a whole, this deck is commonly regarded to have imagery that represents Christian and spiritual figures. During the Renaissance, the mix of images represented in this deck was somewhat radical. With Christian imagery such as The Devil and The Pope alongside more forward-thinking figures like *La Papesse*, the fictional "female pope," this deck sparked controversy.

Rider-Waite Tarot Deck

This is likely the most recognized and famous tarot deck today. Modern tarot decks still take inspiration from and mirror the Rider-Waite deck's artwork.

In the early twentieth century, spiritualist A. E. Waite paired up with artist Pamela Coleman Smith to create a comprehensive tarot deck that would take the British occult world by storm. The deck was published by the Rider Company in 1909.

Smith never received proper recognition for her artwork, so the Smith-Waite tarot deck was created to honor her in 2009. Even so, you can see her initials inscribed in the lower right-hand corner of every card.

Thoth Deck

The Thoth deck was published in 1944 by British occultist Aleister Crowley, who took inspiration from Egyptian myth and history. While his tarot deck was based on Rider-Waite, the artwork contains many references to astrology and alchemy. Among other deviations, the Thoth deck represents Temperance as "Art," Pentacles as "Discs," and Pages as "Princesses."

Crowley also published his own version of the *Book of Thoth*, which is a guidebook meant to be sold with the deck. It is important to recognize that the tarot cards we use today were designed during British imperialism in Egypt—developed in the throes of colonialism. Thus, Egyptian symbols such as sphinxes appear in such decks. Though Crowley draws from Egyptian myth and symbolism, the deck was also designed using Christian imagery and reflects a colonizer's view of the world in many ways.

An Overview of the Major Arcana

Both the Major and Minor Arcana are extremely important. They are two sides of the same coin; you can't have one without the other. That said, the Major Arcana holds more elevated spiritual significance (a "big picture" view), while the Minor holds more day-to-day significance (a "small picture" view).

In fact, the word "arcana" means "mysteries" or "secrets," so one could translate the Minor and Major to "minor secrets" and "major secrets." Thinking about it that way, the Minor Arcana will appear when unlocking trivial ideas or concepts. But the Major Arcana will only reveal itself when it has something prominent to say.

The Major Arcana is a twenty-two-card section of the tarot deck that discusses big life changes, major chapter moments, spiritual moments, and foundational themes.

This section of the tarot deck starts with The Fool (0) and ends with The World (XXI). The order of this section represents something we call "the Fool's journey"—which is similar to a "hero's journey." The main character in any book or movie starts out oblivious to what is to come; then they endure trials, excitement, and love. Inevitably, by the end of the story, they have developed greatly.

We are all experiencing multiple life cycles at one time. For example, if we are starting a new career path, we may associate the Fool card with where we are at in our career journey. On the other hand, we may be at The World in the realm of love, about to get married and start a new chapter of our love life.

An Overview of the Minor Arcana

The fifty-six cards of the Minor Arcana represent more minute and day-to-day emotions, interactions, movements, and experiences.

This section is set up similarly to a deck of playing cards. There are four suits, a numbered section starting with Ace and running through ten, and a court card system. The main thing that makes the Minor Arcana different from a deck of playing cards is the Jack in the court card system being gendered—bringing the total card count from fifty-two cards to fifty-six cards. The "feminine" Jack is called a Page, and the "masculine" Jack is called a Knight.

The Minor Arcana is different from the Major Arcana because it explores life through a daily lens. For example, when you feel excited to go on a date, annoyed that someone cut you off on the road, or betrayed by a friend who canceled on you again, those are all experiences and feelings that will come up in the Minor Arcana.

Suits

The four suits—Wands, Cups, Swords, and Pentacles—will signify the type of experience you're having. For example, feeling let down by a friend who flaked is an emotional moment and would therefore be represented by a Cups card. Getting cut off on the road would be represented by a Swords card, because it involves action.

Here are a few keywords to associate with the four suits:

Wands: thoughts, goals, dreams, visions of the future, hope, passion

Cups: feelings, emotions, sensitivities, memories, connections, relationships, love, romance

Swords: intellect, logic, action, motivation, purpose

Pentacles: money, career, domesticity, body, family, energy

Court Cards

The court cards—Page, Knight, Queen, and King—typically symbolize people that we interact with. The suit associated with the court card will give you more information as to who this person is.

When learning, it's important to recognize that the gendered aspects of the court cards do not need to reflect the genders of people you may be thinking about in real life. For example, when you see a King of Cups card appear in a spread, that card is associated with masculine, mature energy. Though you can certainly relate that card to an older male figure, it could also represent a mature figure of any gender and age. The difference between court cards just comes down to sensitivity and maturity. One of the best ways to memorize these cards is to associate each one with an actual person you know.

Here are a few keywords for the court cards:

Page: feminine, immature, naive, caring, empathetic, humble

Knight: masculine, immature, naive, self-starting, risk-taking, confident (potentially arrogant)

Queen: feminine, mature, nurturing, sensitive, giving

King: masculine, mature, willful, stubborn, powerful

Numbers

The numbered system in the Minor Arcana suggests feelings, actions, and experiences. Identify what each number represents and apply it to the suit. For example, since Fives symbolize instability or chaos, and Cups symbolize emotions, the Five of Cups can be a time of loss, grief, or breakups.

Here are a few keywords for each of the numbers:

Ace/One: new beginnings, fresh starts

Two: duality, decisions, choices, relationships

Three: teamwork, ideas, inspiration

Four: foundation, stability, success

Five: instability, chaos, challenges

Six: respite, accomplishment

Seven: illusion, deception, tests

Eight: progress, movement, power

Nine: cycles, dreams, isolation

Ten: completion, fulfillment, endings (and new beginnings)

COLORS + SYMBOLS

If you can believe it, there's even *more* to tarot than the imagery and numbers on each card. As you use your deck more frequently, you will start to notice some recurring themes that pop up in the deck, such as colors and symbols. This is more than just a coincidence; these two elements can help you identify card meanings and overall themes of the deck you are using.

While every tarot deck is different, most decks will have their own color palette. These colors are meant to evoke the feelings that each card portrays. For example, the color red may be used for cards that represent a betrayal of trust or deception. It's up to the reader to identify how each of the deck's colors make them feel and find their recurring patterns.

Symbols and motifs are incredibly important as well. Traditionally, the recurring symbols in the tarot deck (aside from the suits, of course) include the infinity symbol, the moon or the sun, mountains, sunflowers, birds, and the zodiac symbols (the bull, the lion, etc.).

Many of the symbols you see in the tarot cards connect back to astrology. For example, most of the Swords court card family depict birds in the background as a testament to air signs (Libra, Gemini, Aquarius), which are ruled by Swords. The Strength card is often depicted with a woman taming a lion, which is Leo's astrological symbol.

The 22 Major Arcana Cards

THE FOOL

THE MAGICIAN

THE FOOL (0) represents the very beginning of a new journey or new chapter in your life. It appears when you're experimenting with exciting opportunities that you've never tried before.

THE MAGICIAN (I) represents a time of preparedness and confidence. The card depicts all four suits of the tarot deck, a representation of having all the tools you need for success.

THE HIGH PRIESTESS

THE EMPRESS

THE HIGH PRIESTESS (II) indicates a moment of consciousness and connection with your intuition. When it appears, it's a signal to listen to the little voice inside your head.

THE EMPRESS (III) represents worth in all its aspects. This includes material worth, beauty, and self-worth. Ultimately, the card encourages you to find your own personal value.

THE EMPEROR

THE HIEROPHANT

THE EMPEROR (IV) indicates something of the opposite of his feminine counterpart. This card indicates materialism and finding power in leadership.

THE HIEROPHANT (V) symbolizes the foundations that you grew up with, such as religion, spirituality, family values, and traditions. It represents the core of who you are.

THE LOVERS

THE CHARIOT

THE LOVERS (VI) shows two people deep in passion and lust. This card really represents the excitement of lust and new love, which may not last as long as a marriage or long-term commitment.

THE CHARIOT (VII) indicates a time when you're asked to choose your heart's desires. There is often a "heart versus head" decision associated with this card.

STRENGTH (VIII) symbolizes a period of extreme self-confidence, determination, and willpower. When it appears, it's a sign that you should draw encouragement from the self.

THE HERMIT (IX) indicates a moment of personal progression and self-betterment. It depicts a person in solitude, but this person is choosing to be alone so they can truly find themselves.

THE WHEEL OF FORTUNE (X) indicates luck (good or bad) and spontaneous events. The thing with this card is that the Wheel is associated with fate or karma. It all comes back around . . .

JUSTICE (XI) suggests a time of fairness or abiding by expectations or social structures. Mostly, this card is about how much responsibility you carry around and the expectations put upon you.

THE HANGED MAN (XII) represents a time when you're finding a way to reconcile with the darker parts of yourself. It can act as a reality check for those who avoid change.

DEATH (XIII) suggests a time of change, evolution, and new beginnings. This card signifies the end of a chapter, but that also means there's a new beginning ahead.

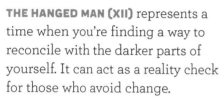

TEMPERANCE (XIV) shows an angel balancing two cups in synchronicity. For that reason, it indicates a time when you're staying emotionally level and finding moderation in life.

THE DEVIL (XV) represents materialism or a toxic relationship you have with something. This could refer to relationships with yourself, partners, substances, etc. It suggests negative cycles in all respects, including negative self-talk.

THE TOWER (XVI) signifies a time of chaos and irreparable damage. While many find this card intimidating, The Tower only brings down what wasn't working in our life.

THE STAR (XVII) suggests a time of ultimate hope, dreams, and expansion. It represents dreaming without limits or expectations.

THE MOON (XVIII) depicts the moon in the sky as an enchanting symbol. It's a card of escapism, disconnect, and secrets that are coming to the surface.

THE SUN (XIX) represents optimism, happiness, and fulfillment. With a child depicted here, the card is also a symbol of family or children (think of how optimistic children are).

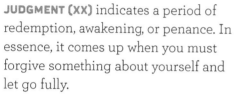

JUDGMENT (XX) indicates a period of redemption, awakening, or penance. In essence, it comes up when you must forgive something about yourself and let go fully.

THE WORLD (XXI) signifies endings, fulfillment, and new chapters ahead. Just like the Death card, The World doesn't mean "endings" necessarily. It indicates excitement for the future.

The 56 Minor Arcana Cards

Cups

ACE OF CUPS

2 OF CUPS

THE ACE OF CUPS symbolizes new relationships, exciting connections, and brand-new love. Optimism and hope are important for this card, as it's focused on the present as opposed to the future.

THE TWO OF CUPS is the ultimate true love card in the deck. It shows a bond that overcomes all obstacles using the power of passion, determination, and desire.

3 OF CUPS

4 OF CUPS

THE THREE OF CUPS card shows three people in a socializing mood—which is exactly what this card represents: connection, friends, and "three's a crowd." However, it may point to issues with boundaries in relationships.

THE FOUR OF CUPS indicates a time when you're contemplating your feelings, before you make efforts to act on them. This card can represent the ultimate form of moodiness.

THE FIVE OF CUPS is a blatant display of pain and grief. This card indicates the process of going through a really tough time and finding closure or recovery from emotional loss.

THE SIX OF CUPS represents memories and the past. As seen with the children in this card, it often represents young people, childhood, and childhood friends or young lovers.

THE SEVEN OF CUPS is a card of emotional deception and illusion. It appears when your heart wants something to work so badly that you end up missing red flags.

THE EIGHT OF CUPS represents letting go and moving on. The card depicts someone leaving broken Cups behind, symbolic of leaving behind something that has hit a dead end.

9 OF CUPS

10 OF CUPS

THE NINE OF CUPS suggests a dreamlike happiness or a time when wishes are fulfilled. It's a period of ultimate bliss.

THE TEN OF CUPS indicates a time when dreams come true, and you feel emotionally fulfilled. As it relates to dreams, relationships, and personal happiness, it can't get better than this.

PAGE OF CUPS

KNIGHT OF CUPS

THE PAGE OF CUPS suggests someone with feminine energy who is artistic, giving, and humble. They know how to tap into their creativity and often give too much.

THE KNIGHT OF CUPS represents someone with masculine energy who is sensitive, passionate, and hopeful. This person is a romantic at heart but may take some time to warm up.

QUEEN OF CUPS

KING OF CUPS

THE QUEEN OF CUPS is a mature, feminine caregiver who enjoys helping others and being that shoulder to cry on. Think about the person who is always looking out for everyone else's needs in the friend group.

THE KING OF CUPS indicates an individual with a mature, masculine energy who is mysterious and deeply engaging. They know how to embody (and control) their passions.

Pentacles

ACE OF PENTACLES

2 OF PENTACLES

THE ACE OF PENTACLES represents the beginning of a new material chapter such as buying a house or starting a new job. It brings a sense of excitement for long-term opportunities.

THE TWO OF PENTACLES symbolizes feeling overwhelmed by multiple material obligations at once. A person juggling two Pentacles is depicted representing the many responsibilities one must look after.

3 OF PENTACLES

4 OF PENTACLES

THE THREE OF PENTACLES shows a time of building and progress. It typically aims to encourage teamwork between parties of three or more.

THE FOUR OF PENTACLES signifies establishing structure or foundation among material things. Depending on how this card is presented, it can indicate success or greed.

5 OF PENTACLES

6 OF PENTACLES

THE FIVE OF PENTACLES depicts loss and poverty. The sadness of the card carries feelings of worthlessness and hopelessness.

THE SIX OF PENTACLES, as shown in the card, symbolizes a time of charity—whether you're giving or receiving it. It brings with it a sense of abundance in the material world.

7 OF PENTACLES

8 OF PENTACLES

THE SEVEN OF PENTACLES is a card of patience. Typically, it indicates a time when you're waiting for your time to shine, but it can also signify a standstill, suggesting that you need to act.

THE EIGHT OF PENTACLES represents a period of determination and hard work. As shown in the card, there's a sheer determination to complete our goal.

9 OF PENTACLES

10 OF PENTACLES

THE NINE OF PENTACLES appears as a symbol of self-worth, success, and abundance. It can suggest not only that you value the things you have in your life, but also that you value yourself.

THE TEN OF PENTACLES suggests a time of complete fulfillment in the material world. If you can picture your perfect life, this card represents that.

PAGE OF PENTACLES

KNIGHT OF PENTACLES

THE PAGE OF PENTACLES represents someone with feminine energy who is exceptionally innovative and ready to take on new projects. This person may be a genius, but they are often humble and grounded.

THE KNIGHT OF PENTACLES suggests a person with masculine energy who puts work above play at all costs. This person is the epitome of the saying, "Slow and steady wins the race."

QUEEN OF PENTACLES

KING OF PENTACLES

THE QUEEN OF PENTACLES indicates someone with a feminine, mature energy who values themself and others. This individual overflows with benevolence.

THE KING OF PENTACLES symbolizes someone with masculine, mature energy who is powerful, structured, and traditional. This person may also be stuck in their ways.

Swords

ACE OF SWORDS

2 OF SWORDS

THE ACE OF SWORDS indicates a time of exciting new starts, bold moves, and innovative new projects. This card usually represents something that you've never done before.

THE TWO OF SWORDS shows two swords crossing one another—which symbolizes contradictory actions or mixed signals.

3 OF SWORDS

4 OF SWORDS

THE THREE OF SWORDS symbolizes a time of betrayal or distrust. This card always refers to some level of boundaries being crossed within relationships or connections.

THE FOUR OF SWORDS shows a person lying still or at peace. For that reason, it indicates a period of rest or patience. It encourages thinking before acting.

THE FIVE OF SWORDS suggests a time when you're distancing or cutting yourself off from relationships that no longer serve you. With it comes a cold but self-preserving attitude.

THE SIX OF SWORDS shows individuals sailing away on a boat. This card symbolizes letting go of, moving on from, or finding peace with the past.

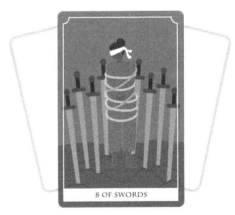

THE SEVEN OF SWORDS represents a time when secrets are being hidden or revealed. In general, it brings a sense of hiding or deception.

THE EIGHT OF SWORDS shows a woman blindfolded with many swords around her. She sees what she wants to see, making this a card that symbolizes feeling trapped or glossing over red flags.

9 OF SWORDS

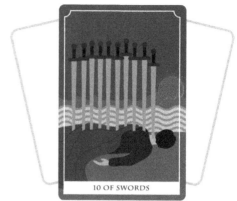

10 OF SWORDS

THE NINE OF SWORDS is often referred to as the "nightmare card" for its connection to anxiety, overthinking, and worry. Consider it symbolic of the darker places your mind can go.

THE TEN OF SWORDS symbolizes a time when your actions are coming back to haunt you. It can indicate karmic retribution, feelings of failure, or a dead end.

PAGE OF SWORDS

KNIGHT OF SWORDS

THE PAGE OF SWORDS represents someone with feminine energy who is bold, independent, and a powerful fighter. This person feels they are more successful on their own than with a group.

THE KNIGHT OF SWORDS represents an individual with masculine energy who is spontaneous and ambitious. As a self-starter, this person knows what they want and isn't afraid to take risks.

THE QUEEN OF SWORDS symbolizes someone mature, who has feminine energy and enjoys planning. They prefer to stay emotionally aloof, allowing them to speak fairly on any topic.

THE KING OF SWORDS symbolizes a person with mature, masculine energy who is calculated and logical. This person is a natural leader, and they are able to guide others with a forceful hand.

Wands

THE ACE OF WANDS signifies new ideas, plans, or dreams. The depiction of a singular Wand is meant to show one brilliant new path going forward.

THE TWO OF WANDS represents a time when your ideas are in alignment with the world around you or another person. In essence, it shows progress and an overall plan for the future.

THE THREE OF WANDS indicates a time of visualization and dreaming about the future. It encourages you to dream without limits or borders.

THE FOUR OF WANDS suggests a time when the plans you've put in place are manifesting in the real world. It indicates success and pride in what you've accomplished.

THE FIVE OF WANDS shows fights or feelings of imbalance. Since Wands represent dreams and thoughts, this card can appear when you're overthinking or disagreeing with someone.

THE SIX OF WANDS represents a time of success, pride, and power. It depicts a congratulatory moment—embodying the motto that if you believe it, you can achieve it.

7 OF WANDS

8 OF WANDS

THE SEVEN OF WANDS depicts the moment when will and determination meet success (or failure). This card encourages you to fight for your dreams and opinions—even if they end up being wrong.

THE EIGHT OF WANDS is a card of striking inspiration and enlightenment. Think of it as an end to writer's block or the moment you finally land on a million-dollar idea.

9 OF WANDS

10 OF WANDS

THE NINE OF WANDS signifies a time of resilience and keeping faith. It can either encourage you to continue moving forward or ask you to reconsider the plan.

THE TEN OF WANDS, like most Ten cards, represents fulfillment. In this case, it indicates finally reaching your dreams and manifesting your ideal life.

THE PAGE OF WANDS represents someone with feminine energy who has big dreams, great excitement, and unbridled passion. This person is a true visionary and can look at things from an artistic perspective.

THE KNIGHT OF WANDS depicts a person with masculine energy who is opinionated, energetic, and very positive. They will fight tooth and nail for what they believe.

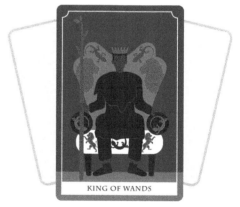

THE QUEEN OF WANDS signifies someone with mature, feminine energy who is thoughtful and grounded in their goals. However, this person typically has a feisty side.

KING OF WANDS shows a mature individual with masculine energy who is inspiring, expansive, and proud. This person has such charisma that they can truly make you believe in the impossible.

KEY TAKEAWAYS

Before we get started, here's a little recap. The modern tarot deck—the one we know and recognize today—most commonly reflects the artwork and symbolism of the Rider-Waite tarot deck, published in 1910. There are two types of divinatory cards out there: tarot and oracle. This workbook has been written under the assumption that you'll be working with a tarot deck.

Every tarot deck has two sections: a Major Arcana (twenty-two cards) and a Minor Arcana (fifty-six cards). The Major Arcana represents more life-changing or spiritual themes. The Minor Arcana represents in-the-moment feelings, experiences, people, and desires.

♦ Tarot is a unique divinatory tool because it promotes direct communication with your most authentic self.

♦ Recurring themes like colors and symbols pop up in every deck. These can help you identify card meanings.

♦ The four suits—Wands, Cups, Swords, and Pentacles—signify types of experiences.

♦ The court cards—Page, Knight, Queen, and King—typically symbolize people.

♦ The Minor Arcana has a numbered system. Each number is associated with feelings, actions, and experiences.

CHAPTER 2

PRACTICING TAROT FOR PERSONAL GROWTH

You might be thinking, "Isn't tarot just a pack of cards?" While this may be true, that pack of cards has the capability to help you tap into so much more insight than you might expect. Tarot can offer an intuitive look into the next six months, guidance on whether to take that job, or a definitive "yes" or "no" regarding Jack's feelings for you. But this is all surface-level stuff: What if you could take tarot deeper? What if you could do more with it than simply glean the answers that your ego needs and, instead, soak in more therapeutic and revealing knowledge about the self?

When used correctly, tarot can open your mind to places that you may not willingly go to on your own. That's because when you choose to go deeper into the subconscious alone, you don't have the support you need to fully accept the messages. But when you dive in with an uplifting tool such as tarot, you are more willing to hear the truth. Consider tarot an extension of your most trusted and accessible personal therapist: you.

In this chapter, we'll cover why tarot is an amazing self-growth tool and how you can use it to your highest advantage.

Looking to Tarot as a Teacher

When we face any issue, we are typically up against more than a simple problem. In fact, there are three components to any problem:

◆ The core issue

◆ Inside influences

◆ Outside influences

The core issue is the problem or question at face value. Inside influences might involve things like personal pressure, ethics, and the classic "head versus heart" dilemma. And outside influences might involve things like societal pressure, location, or the feelings or perspectives of others involved.

Tarot is a unique tool that can mold itself into a conduit for considering these three components. When you use tarot, you employ three tools: intuition, problem-solving skills, and a fresh perspective. Here is a breakdown of how each tool interacts with the three components of a problem.

Intuition + core issue: Your intuition is that gut feeling you get as you draw the cards. This instinct allows you to make an initial pass on the core issue—whether it aligns with your values, how you feel initially, etc.

Problem-solving skills + inside influences: Because tarot comes in fragments, it encourages you to learn how to connect the dots on your own. In doing so, you're not only learning how to piece together the problem, but you're exploring the *root* of the problem and the extra forces that make it more difficult for you personally.

Fresh perspective + outside influences: Because tarot is an outside object, its advice naturally comes from a different point of view. Because of this, it allows you to see things from a new perspective before making decisions.

How Tarot Enables and Encourages Growth

Personal growth is a challenge. In order to grow, you have to face truths that are not always easy to hear. Fortunately, tarot doesn't share the same sensitivities. As a third-party tool, it has the distinct ability to present what you *need* to hear so you're able to make the best decisions for the future.

With a tarot deck, the journey to the core is much more streamlined. It allows you to tap into your deepest self, without the uncomfortable feeling of getting too up close and personal. That's why tarot is such a special tool for self-growth: It not only provides the safe space you need to be vulnerable, it also provides the privacy you wouldn't have when sharing your thoughts with someone else.

Tarot is very matter-of-fact in its responses, but it also allows us to see situations (and ourselves) from a different point of view. With that in mind, tarot offers either reassurance or new perspectives. For example, after I give someone a reading they might say, "That's what I've been thinking all along!"—which suggests that I've offered them reassurance. Or, they might say, "I hadn't thought about it that way before," indicating that I've offered a new perspective. Basically, tarot helps us locate where we've been thinking correctly or where we may need to view things differently. Because its answers are direct, it becomes a straightforward way to approach self-development.

Areas of Focus for Your Personal Growth Practice

"Growth" can mean something different for every individual. While we may all be working on ourselves, in what way and to what degree is a very individualistic thing. In order to connect with as many people as possible, I've developed eight areas of focus that capture every part of life:

1. Self-knowledge and self-love
2. Where you are and where you want to go
3. Mental and emotional well-being
4. Social life and community
5. Love and romance
6. Work and prosperity
7. Hardship resolution
8. Manifesting joy and resilience

The exercises in part 2 of this book are organized according to these areas of focus, because approaching self-progression in segments can help make the growth process more manageable. Additionally, it gives you the freedom to personalize your path and work on any section of your life that requires a little more TLC than others.

Self-Knowledge and Self-Love

Self-knowledge refers to understanding who you are as an individual. When we know ourselves—our morals, opinions, viewpoints, personality, and ego—we can more easily focus on connecting with the underdeveloped parts of ourselves. Consider this similar to the "getting to know you" stage on a first date.

While self-knowledge is more like a first date, self-love refers to what happens after. It's about actively improving the relationship you have with yourself. Do you treat yourself with kindness? Respect? This point of interest activates self-respect, self-worth, and self-confidence in relation to the world around you.

Where You Are and Where You Want to Go

When discussing "where you are" currently, we don't just mean physically. This location could be geographic, spiritual, or in respect to the goals or dreams you have for yourself. This is the section of the workbook where you'll get real about what you like and don't like about your entire life right now.

The second part of this section, "where you want to go," will piggyback on the previous part. We'll dive into any current desires and find ways to expand on them. This section will inspire you, encourage you, and expand your way of thinking about what you can accomplish.

Mental and Emotional Well-Being

The mental well-being section allows you to examine your mindset. Is it in a healthy, self-loving place? Or does it need a rearrangement or some form of rewiring? This section tackles mental obstacles such as anxiety, perfectionism, negative thought patterns, and people-pleasing.

Emotional well-being refers to gauging the status of your emotional life. Are your emotions balanced? Do you have a healthy relationship with your various feelings? Do you even know what you're feeling? This section tackles emotional obstacles such as feeling overwhelmed, fears of failure, childhood experiences, and personal boundaries.

Social Life and Community

We live in a relational world, so we tend to view ourselves with respect to the world around us. For example, success at work might mean that we're succeeding more than our fellow coworkers. Having a lot of acquaintances might make us feel less lonely. This section of the workbook will help you realign yourself with *you*, not just the world around you.

Using tarot's objective point of view, you will be able to plainly address social and community obstacles such as relationships with friends, family pressure, and interpersonal or social skills.

Love and Romance

Relationships, the thrill of falling in love, and the pursuit of romance can be exciting, energizing, and . . . utterly confusing. This section covers information about how you approach and relate to partnerships, regardless of your relationship status.

We'll use the cards to uncover relationship patterns, personal triggers, existing baggage from previous connections, how to best approach love, and where you might find love next. For those who are partnered, you'll use tarot to discuss the status of your relationship, how to better understand your partner, and which areas need attention in order for relationships to grow.

Work and Prosperity

As mentioned, we live in a relational world. This often means that we place a certain level of pressure on ourselves to be the same as or better than those around us. For some, the concept of prosperity means having the ability to pay for the same things as your friend. Sometimes the desire for prosperity motivates our work and informs what we consider "working hard."

This section aims to uncover whether your approach to work is healthy, how you view success, and the natural skills or talents you have that will lead you to your desires. In general, this section redefines success by addressing what you want personally, as opposed to what you feel you're supposed to want based on societal, family, or personal pressures.

Overcoming Hardships

Tarot is a fabulous tool to help find closure in tough situations. But everyone is different, and everyone's *situation* is different. To one person, a breakup might mean the end of the world, whereas to another it presents opportunities. This section provides the foundational tools you need to overcome these hardships. Many general exercises are included that can apply to any situation. However, there will be a few exercises that correspond to specific situations such as separations and divorce, death, and general loss.

Manifesting Joy and Resilience

Elements of life like work, love, and family are difficult to enjoy if you aren't feeling overall fulfilled. What happens when you can't find happiness no matter how hard you try? What do you do when you feel you are lacking the motivation to keep moving forward?

This section tackles those concerns by providing tarot exercises for motivation, inspiration, and happiness. It encourages you to consider what inspires you, where you can find more encouragement in your life, how to create a more fulfilling daily routine, and how to bring gratitude into your life.

Preparing to Get Started

I know you're excited to get started, but before you do, there are a few things you can do that will help you get the most out of this workbook. This includes how to prepare your deck for readings and how to best connect with your deck as you read.

These preparations are merely extra steps to help you receive messages faster and with more clarity. But they aren't a one-size-fits-all recipe. Whether you practice them or not, tarot will still guide you. As you look through the preparation ideas, determine which ones are a good fit for you. It's totally acceptable if one of the preparations is outside your comfort zone or doesn't feel right for you. Tarot is a personalized self-help tool, so anything you do with your deck should make sense to you and feel right on a personal level.

In addition to deck and reading preparation techniques, this section also includes a primer on how to actively interpret messages your cards present to you. Finally, we will cover how to continue the reflection process days after you've pulled the spread.

Readying Your Deck

While all tarot decks are essentially the same, the one that you use must be a deck that you resonate with. There are so many styles and kinds of artwork out there—from cat decks to ones portraying literary heroes. So, there's definitely a deck out there for you. Before you begin this journey, take some time to pick out a deck that "speaks" to you on a personal level. You could feel connected to the artwork, the symbolism, or even the colors. Whatever works.

Once you have a deck that you feel connected to, it's time to get the deck ready for readings. There are a few ways you can prep the deck so it will immediately start working for you. First, make sure all the cards are present. I've experienced a few instances where I've started shuffling and later realized that the cards from my previous reading were on another table. Tarot works best when all cards are accounted for.

Secondly, you should cleanse or "clear" your deck before use to detox the tarot deck of any lingering energy from previous readings. There are a few ways to cleanse a deck, but my favorite is to simply place a clear quartz crystal on the top of it. Allow the deck to sit with the quartz for a minimum of one hour before use. If you don't have a clear quartz crystal on hand, you can clear your deck by placing it in a bag, filling a bowl with salt (an energy cleanser), and letting the deck rest in the salt for an hour or more.

Connecting to the Cards

Tarot cards are rich with color, symbolism, and personal meaning. They evoke feelings, experiences, and expressions that are individual to every person. With this in mind, it's useful to create a personal relationship with your tarot deck before you begin any reading.

Yes, it's a thing. Get up close and personal with your cards. The closer you feel to your tarot deck, the more detailed the answers you will receive.

The best way to build a relationship with your deck is by pulling the cards out one by one and analyzing them. Feel free to use a paper and pen to document what you see or how you feel about each card. In general, this should give you a couple of keywords to immediately connect with.

Speaking to Your Cards

This may seem strange, but it's common practice for tarot readers to "interview" the cards when they receive a new deck. This is called an interview tarot reading.

Create the spread in whatever way you like. Here are some sample questions to ask:

- What topic do you most enjoy reading about?

- What are your strengths and weaknesses?

- What can you teach me?

- In what way can you be misunderstood?

- How can I best connect with you?

- How can we work together most productively?

- What card defines you as a tarot deck?

- Are there any messages you'd like to give me?

Interpreting Your Cards

The best advice: Go with what your gut says. As you pull cards, note how you feel when you see each one. There are many times when I pull a card and instinctively feel that *this time* the card means something different than the meaning that I would normally apply to it.

Note that if a card flies out of the deck spontaneously, this is called a flier card. Use the flier card as a theme card for the reading. If you're shuffling and a card leaps out of the deck in a prominent way, whether it's showing or not, it's a literal message flying out at you.

Reflecting on Your Cards

As you pull your cards, sit with them for a minute. The worst thing you can do is stress over the fact that there are so many in front of you. Just try to go through the cards one by one. Determine their meanings, take a mental note, and move forward. If you don't rush yourself, the pieces of the puzzle will come together, slowly but surely.

You can take more time to process a reading if you take a picture of your tarot spread. Sometimes, when you pause and look back on a reading, the message becomes abundantly clearer.

A NOTE ON THE SPREADS IN THIS BOOK

Tarot spreads are predetermined layouts for the cards. Each tarot spread specifies the number of cards to be drawn, the questions they are supposed to answer, and the way in which they are laid out. Placement and questions all dictate how the cards are meant to be read. For example, a card that is meant to represent something that blocks you from moving forward might be placed over another, literally and figuratively blocking it.

A good tarot spread will not only answer the main question being asked but also delve deeper into what else you need to know to truly understand the answer to that question. An example of this might be the question "Should we break up?" You can certainly answer this question with a simple pull. But wouldn't it also be helpful to include questions like "What works/doesn't work about this relationship?" and "What's the real reason I'm considering leaving?"

In part 2 of this workbook, certain exercises will incorporate tarot spreads to help you learn how to connect the dots yourself. Some spreads will be quite simple while others will be a little more complex. If you're stumped by the complex spreads (there can be a lot of cards all at once), feel free to start with the smaller spreads and work your way up. I also included exercises that encourage you to create your own tarot spreads as a method of self-exploration.

Setting Clear Intentions as You Journey Forward

Reading tarot without clear intentions is like attempting to follow a map that's been soiled by water stains. You may get the general idea, but all the details are lost.

Whenever I shuffle the cards, I always end up repeating the questions of the spread in my head or out loud. That's not just so I can remember what we're pulling for; it's also for the cards themselves. I believe that tarot cards are their own individual entity. When we ask them questions, we need to be very direct about what we're asking and in what order. They need to clearly understand our questions in order to answer us properly.

Another reason I repeat those questions when I shuffle is to prevent my own mind from wandering during the reading. We all have things that we stress over or worry about. If we're not careful, those anxieties could easily end up in a reading for something else. If you're not careful, the cards might end up answering questions about anxieties in your relationship when you meant to ask about impressing your boss.

To begin this process and practice setting clear intentions, I encourage you to set intentions related to the areas of focus that have been outlined in this book (page 35). Take a few minutes right now to consider what your goals are for these topics.

KEY TAKEAWAYS

In this chapter, we explored how tarot can support your self-growth journey. Tarot can open your mind to places you may not willingly go to on your own. Using tarot allows us to employ intuition, problem-solving skills, and a fresh perspective. These tools help us tackle and understand the many components that comprise any problem.

We also reviewed the areas of focus that will be highlighted in this workbook: self-knowledge and self-love, where you are and where you want to go, mental and emotional well-being, social life and community, love and romance, work and prosperity, overcoming hardships, and manifesting joy and resilience.

To help you prepare for your self-growth journey, you can use techniques to ready your deck and better connect with the cards. You can also find ways to continue processing your tarot reading even after it's over.

◆ Tarot is a key tool for self-growth because it provides a fresh, third-party perspective.

◆ Building a relationship with your deck will help you interpret answers more clearly.

◆ Tarot spreads are detailed card layouts used to answer questions.

◆ If a card flies out of the deck spontaneously (a flier), you can use it as a theme card for the reading.

◆ It is important to be direct and intentional with your questions for the cards.

PART II

Tarot Exercises for Personal Growth

Now that we've covered how tarot can be used for personal growth, it's time to apply these practices to your own life. This workbook is organized into eight sections, each with a specific theme. The first three sections are focused on inner work (self-knowledge and self-love; where you are and where you want to go; and mental and emotional well-being). Next, we will focus on outer community and relationships (social life and community; love and romance; and work and prosperity). Finally, we will explore exercises devoted to specific challenges (overcoming hardships and manifesting joy and resilience).

There is no right or wrong way to approach these categories, but I would suggest starting at the beginning with chapter 3, which focuses on the self. It can be valuable to look inward first since our inner self informs our perspective on the world. If you work on the inner challenges first, you will elevate your ability to handle external challenges.

To get the most out of this workbook experience, remember that each exercise has a specific purpose or lesson. Move slowly and with intention.

CHAPTER 3

SELF-KNOWLEDGE AND SELF-LOVE

In this section of the workbook, we'll approach tarot through the lens of the person who knows you best: you. Getting to know yourself may seem like an easy task, but self-knowledge can be tough. Because of how inherently close we are to ourselves, it can be hard to view the self through an objective lens.

That's where tarot comes in. Tarot is the ultimate mirroring tool to help you gather more information about who you are. This third-party perspective allows you to see, without confrontation, areas for self-improvement, as well as positive attributes and strengths. Though this section may shine a light on things you don't like about yourself, remember that these exercises are not meant to knock you down or find flaws. Think of them as opportunities to be real and vulnerable with yourself.

The exercises in this section will help you learn more about who you are now, how you came to be this way, and how to continue learning about yourself. Through this process, you can build a healthier relationship with yourself.

Color-Me-Pretty: The Empress

Coloring a card in is one of the best ways to learn about it. I know this seems like an unusual tactic, but there is a method to this madness. Every tarot card has a basic picture and scene; however, there can be a vast number of smaller symbols embedded in the card's design. The style of art and color palette can also have an emotive effect on the card reader. Coloring a card in really allows you to connect deeply with the card in front of you.

Now, why The Empress? To me, this card is the epitome of self-love and self-worth. She represents our ability to set boundaries, embrace self-respect, and maintain positive and healthy relationships with ourselves and others.

First, let's ask: What does The Empress mean to you? Pull The Empress card out of your deck. Take a look at her and reflect on what you see. How is she looking at you? How is she dressed? How does she present herself? What does she exude upon first glance? As you analyze the card, write down a few adjectives that remind you of "Empress energy."

_____

_____

_____

_____

_____

_____

_____

_____

Next, color in The Empress using only colors that remind you of the keywords above. As you color, take note of any symbols and facial expressions you hadn't noticed before.

THE EMPRESS

Blind Spot Tarot Spread

This is one of my favorite tarot spreads because with only four cards, not only is it super quick and easy, it's also extremely revealing. If you're new to reading tarot, this is one of the best spreads to start with. Because this spread focuses on the one person you should know better than anyone else (you), you will automatically be able to tell whether the spread is on the right track.

This four-card spread helps you gain a little more knowledge about how others see you and how you relate to people. Use this simple exercise whenever you're ready to dive deeper into who you are.

Draw this spread:

Card 1: *The Outside. What you know about yourself and what others can see.*

Card 2: *The Motivation. What you can't see but is driving you.*

Card 3: *The Hidden. What you know about yourself but don't show others.*

Card 4: *The Blind Spot. What you don't see in yourself, but others see in you.*

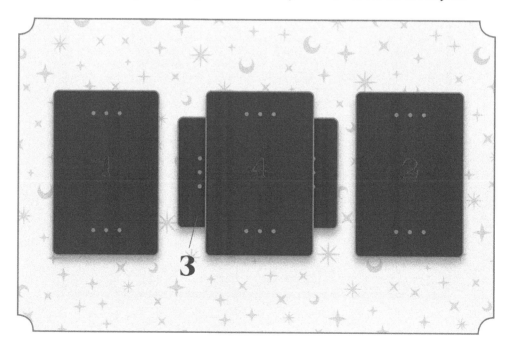

Once you complete the tarot spread, answer a few questions to get even deeper.

Does **Card 1** (The Outside) surprise you? Why or why not?

_____

_____

_____

Would your friends concur that **Card 1** is correct? Why or why not?

_____

_____

_____

Think of your biggest inspiration. How does **Card 2** (The Motivation) relate?

_____

_____

_____

How does **Card 3** (The Hidden) signify something you keep from others? What causes your fears here?

_____

_____

_____

How is **Card 4** (The Blind Spot) surprising? In what ways do you see this appear in your life?

_____

_____

_____

Confidence Boost Tarot Spread

No one can be 100 percent confident all the time. That would be some super-human stuff. This spread helps you recognize that it's totally okay to feel down on yourself every once in a while. In fact, it's extremely common. This tarot spread acts as the trusted bestie that you usually call up in moments when you need a little inspiration or confidence boost.

This spread asks some deep questions, but it also asks some surface-level, almost-egotistical ones. These are questions that many of us are curious about, but would never ask someone. This spread doesn't shy away from the stuff we're afraid to even consider. Overall, the aim of this spread is to help you see the best parts of yourself in ways you hadn't considered before.

This card layout is set up as a pyramid, with each question getting more and more in-depth or revealing as you go forward. This set up is intentional, acting as an aid to help you open up and get comfortable with yourself, building up to the final question.

1. Which card best describes me?

2. What is my greatest quality?

3. What are my natural gifts?

4. What do people love about me?

5. What color looks best on me?

6. How am I different from everyone else?

7. What is something beautiful about me?

8. What's my sexiest quality?

9. What do I love about myself?

10. How would the deck compliment me?

Which Suit Am I? Quiz

Are you motivated by energy and passion? Or do you tend to take a more practical, logical stance on life? This suits quiz identifies elements of your core personality and how it leads you in life, based on the four suits of the tarot deck: Wands, Cups, Swords, and Pentacles.

Circle the answers that best represent you.

1. *When I'm angry, I . . .*

    a. *Lash out and fight back*

    b. *Cry*

    c. *Express my fair-but-direct counterargument*

    d. *Walk away until I know what to say*

2. *When I have a brilliant new idea, I . . .*

    a. *Start envisioning all that could be*

    b. *Ask myself, "Would this fulfill me?"*

    c. *Work on a plan to get it done*

    d. *Take the first step forward to accomplishing it*

3. *When it comes to romantic relationships, I much prefer . . .*

    a. *Quick and fun flings*

    b. *Great sex and emotional chats*

    c. *What's a "relationship"?*

    d. *Long-term partnerships*

4. *Which activity do you enjoy doing most?*

    a. *Sports*

    b. *Beach or pool*

    c. *Taking a course or learning something new*

    d. *Cooking*

5. *Which word best describes you?*

    a. *Spontaneous*

    b. *Caring*

    c. *Unique*

    d. *Loyal*

6. *What's the size of your friend group?*

    a. *Abundant with besties . . . and acquaintances*

    b. *All friends are welcome, but I can only handle the ones who live close*

    c. *About two to four people at a time*

    d. *Three long-term friends from high school*

7. *What is your favorite movie genre?*

    a. *Action*

    b. *Romantic comedy*

    c. *Science fiction or fantasy*

    d. *Drama*

Tally up your answers to find out which suit your personality is associated with.

Mostly As—Wands

A fiery, self-starting, and intense person who is extremely passionate in everything they do. This person may be a little hotheaded or impulsive at times, but it's only because they refuse to live life with boundaries. That said, they need freedom.

CONTINUED >

Mostly Bs—Cups

An empathetic, sensitive, and caring person who gives their heart all at once to the people that they care about. This person is fearless with their heart, has unbridled love to give, and would prefer to open up about everything.

Mostly Cs—Swords

A no-bull, intelligent, and cut-to-the-chase person who won't start the argument but who will win every time. This suit indicates someone who thinks with their head, not their heart, which makes them excellent planners but less so in vulnerability.

Mostly Ds—Pentacles

A practical, traditional, no-frills person who enjoys routine more than anything else. A predictable world is a safe world, and this person lives for that kind of sensible meaning. Additionally, this person is very much a "I'll believe it when I see it" type.

Write down which suit represents you: _____

Shadow + Light

Using tarot as a direct line of contact to your intuition and your core self, you can reveal answers and attributes that you might otherwise shy away from. Perhaps there are parts of yourself that you wouldn't know how to uncover in the first place. This exercise uses the entire deck to expose your light sides and your shadow sides, all at once.

First, hold your tarot deck. Make sure all seventy-eight cards are present. Next, turn the deck over so the cards are facing you. Go through each and every card very carefully, then pick five cards that you enjoy or that resonate with you. These are the "light cards." Next, pick five cards that you don't enjoy or that you find off-putting in some way. These are the "shadow cards." Take your time. Listen to how you feel as you look at each card. Is there shame? Disgust? Happiness? Fear?

Next, write the names of each of your chosen cards:

LIGHT CARDS   SHADOW CARDS

_____   _____

_____   _____

_____   _____

_____   _____

The "light cards" signify qualities that we are very proud of or enjoy about ourselves. The "shadow cards" show qualities that we are fearful of or shameful about within ourselves. Take a minute to reflect on a keyword for each "light card" and "dark card."

CONTINUED >

LIGHT CARD KEYWORDS   SHADOW CARD KEYWORDS

_____   _____

_____   _____

_____   _____

_____   _____

_____   _____

Finally, reflect on how each of the ten cards relates to what you're proud of or shameful about. What do each of the keywords have to do with your pride? What about your fears?

_____

_____

_____

_____

_____

_____

_____

_____

_____

_____

_____

_____

_____

_____

_____

_____

_____

Reversed "Shadow Sides"

Using the "shadow cards" from the previous exercise, this exercise offers a completely different perspective on negative traits that you fear or hide from others.

First, lay the five "shadow cards" in front of you. Stare them down and connect with them. Allow yourself to feel in control, superior to the cards.

Next, reverse the cards one by one by rotating them upside down. (If your reading already includes reversals, use the same process of simply turning the card upside down.)

Look at how the reversed position of each card changes the meaning or allows you to see a silver lining. For example, perhaps you feel that you overthink too much, signified by the Eight of Swords. When you turn the card upside down, what positives do you see? A reversed Eight of Swords may suggest that you're able to help others commit to new paths without having to see the whole picture.

Write a brief note about the meaning of each card and the card's reversed meaning:

Card 1 *meaning:* _____

Reversed meaning: _____

Card 2 *meaning:* _____

Reversed meaning: _____

Card 3 *meaning:* _____

Reversed meaning: _____

Card 4 *meaning:* _____

Reversed meaning: _____

Card 5 *meaning:* _____

Reversed meaning: _____

Astrology + Tarot

What's your sun sign? Did you know that tarot cards are closely related to zodiac signs? Each zodiac sign is associated with four tarot cards—one Major Arcana card and three Minor Arcana cards. This exercise uses your sun sign as a jumping-off point for personality discussions. Here, we'll take you through how to find your sun sign's cards.

As you read through, write the names of your zodiac's four tarot cards:

_____

_____

_____

_____

For the Major Arcana, simply find your zodiac below and circle it:

Aries: *The Emperor IV*

Taurus: *The Hierophant V*

Gemini: *The Lovers VI*

Cancer: *The Chariot VII*

Leo: *Strength VIII*

Virgo: *The Hermit IX*

Libra: *Justice XI*

Scorpio: *Death XIII*

Sagittarius: *Temperance XIV*

Capricorn: *The Devil XV*

Aquarius: *The Star XVII*

Pisces: *The Moon XVIII*

Next, circle the modality of your zodiac sign:

CARDINAL   FIXED   MUTABLE

The modality will determine which section of numbers in the Minor Arcana relate to your sun sign: 2 to 4 (cardinal), 5 to 7 (fixed), or 8 to 10 (mutable).
  Hold that thought . . . we're at the very last step. Circle your sign's element:

FIRE   WATER   AIR   EARTH

The element will determine which suit in the Minor Arcana relates to your sun sign: Wands (fire), Cups (water), Swords (air), or Pentacles (earth).

After that, put it all together. For example, my sun is in Aquarius, a fixed air sign. So, my three Minor Arcana cards are: Five of Swords, Six of Swords, and Seven of Swords. Write down the final three cards in the section on the previous page.

How do your four sun sign cards represent you?

_____

_____

_____

_____

_____

_____

_____

_____

_____

_____

_____

_____

_____

_____

_____

Life Path Number Cards

Numerology is a big part of tarot. The numbers from 1 to 10 all have different meanings. Because tarot consists of numerological cycles in both the Minor Arcana and Major Arcana, all ten numbers appear more than once in the tarot deck.

In numerology, a life path number represents who you are as your core self. This exercise brings tarot and numerology together to show you a few cards that represent your core self. You can find your life path number using your birthday and some simple math.

Write down your birthday. For example: 02/06/1993

Next, add all the numbers in your birthday together. The example would look like this: 2 + 6 + 1 + 9 + 9 + 3 = 30.

If the added number is above ten—which it likely is—you will need to break it down to a single digit. To do that, add the two numbers together again. If the sum of those numbers is still over ten, repeat the same process again until you identify one number. The example above would look like this 30 = 3 + 0 = 3.

Now that you have your life path number, go through the tarot deck and identify every card that relates to your number. There will be five cards total—four from the Minor Arcana and one from the Major Arcana. The example's life path number is three, so I would write down these cards:

- *Three of Wands*

- *Three of Cups*

- *Three of Swords*

- *Three of Pentacles*

- *The Empress (III)*

Write the names of your five life path cards:

_____

_____

_____

_____

_____

Finally, reflect on what these cards say about your core identity.

_____

_____

_____

_____

_____

_____

_____

_____

_____

_____

_____

_____

_____

_____

_____

_____

Self-Love Quiz

We would all like to think that we're good to ourselves, but there might be more to uncover there. This self-love quiz helps you get real about where you stand in your relationship with yourself. After, you can pull a simple spread based on your quiz results.

Circle the answers that best represent you.

1. When someone I love is angry, I automatically wonder what I did to upset them.

    a. True

    b. False

2. I often forget to set boundaries with others.

    a. True

    b. False

3. I am always comparing myself (my body, my accomplishments, etc.) to others.

    a. True

    b. False

4. When I look in the mirror, the first thing I do is pick apart something I don't like about my body.

    a. True

    b. False

5. Everyone else seems to have it together except for me.

    a. True

    b. False

6. *When someone gives me a compliment, I brush it off.*

    a. *True*

    b. *False*

7. *When I make a mistake, I tend to beat myself up over it until I feel better.*

    a. *True*

    b. *False*

8. *When alone, I feel anxious, as though I need to do something or be with others.*

    a. *True*

    b. *False*

9. *When someone criticizes me, I tend to apologize right away and think about how to better myself.*

    a. *True*

    b. *False*

Mostly True—Self-Love Is Needed

Pull cards for these questions and lay them out at random:

> *What does my relationship with myself look like?*
>
> *How do I find more self-love in relation to my body?*
>
> *How do I find more self-love in relation to my core self?*
>
> *What is something I can celebrate about myself that no one else has?*

Mostly False—Self-Love Is Balanced

Pull cards for these questions and lay them out at random:

> *What does my relationship with myself look like?*
>
> *Where could I use a little more self-love in my life?*
>
> *How can I share this self-love with others?*

KEY TAKEAWAYS

Using tarot for self-knowledge can help you understand who you are, how you came to be this way, and where your relationship with yourself currently stands. In learning more about yourself and how much you care for *you*, you can get a better sense of how you present yourself to the world. It can be hard to do this without an objective lens, so tarot acts as an objective mirroring tool.

The most important thing to note is that this section wasn't designed to knock you down or find flaws. These exercises give you a venue to be real with yourself and break down barriers so you can connect with your authentic self: the good, the bad, the not-so-great, and the absolutely amazing. In connecting with these deep insights, I encourage you to try to embrace and enjoy *all* parts of you.

- It is important to connect with every part of you (even the not-so-great parts).

- Tarot is the ultimate mirroring tool, offering an objective, third-party perspective with new insights.

- Tarot doesn't shy away from any topic, good or bad. You can dive deep into the light sides and shadow sides of yourself in a safe environment.

- Numerology and astrology are both closely associated with tarot.

- Learning to love yourself is a key step on the road to self-knowledge.

CHAPTER 4

WHERE YOU ARE AND WHERE YOU WANT TO GO

The exercises in chapter 3 pave a path toward understanding yourself a bit better. This chapter focuses more on the actionable side of things. It asks you to identify who you are today. Where are you starting from? With that in mind, where do you see yourself in the future? Where do you want to take yourself from here? It's time to identify your starting point as well as your goals for the finish line.

Tarot is an ideal tool for recognition and planning. It highlights the ideas in our mind that we have yet to uncover. I believe that deep down, we have all the information we need, but we just may not have access to it. You *know* what you want to do. You *know* how to get from Point A to Point B. You just need a tool to unlock this information for you.

The exercises in this chapter will help you identify who you are, who you were, what your strengths and weaknesses are, what you dream of accomplishing, and what you're already incredibly grateful for. In uncovering these insights, tarot encourages you to both dream big and uncover the next steps toward any goal you desire.

Signifier Card

Selecting a signifier card is a powerful tool for many tarot spreads. When you select a signifier card, you look through the deck with intention related to a specific prompt or person. In this instance, you will be looking for a signifier card that represents *you*. This exercise will help you maintain inspiration about your future and build momentum toward who you want to be.

Go through the deck and find one card that truly resonates with you and that you hope to embody.

For example, if you're hoping to become more conscious about who you are and the type of choices you want to make moving forward, The Hermit would be a fantastic pick for you. If you're hoping to be more attentive to the relationships in your life or attract a positive relationship, the Two of Cups or The Lovers would be good card options (depending on whether you're looking for a fun fling or a long-term relationship).

Once you've identified your signifier card, write it here: _____

Next, set up an altar for your card. Place the card upright either against a wall or in a cardholder. Then, around the card, place crystals that represent the kind of energy the card projects. For instance, if you're connecting to The Empress for her self-love, you might scatter rose quartz stones around the card. It is also helpful to use items that make you feel like the person you're attempting to embody. An example of this for self-love might be a handwritten note from your daughter about how loving and caring you are. Use whatever warms your heart.

Place the card in a spot where you can see it daily. If you can, attempt to place it in a location that connects to the intention. A work intention card might do well on your work desk, for example.

Leave the card there for an entire month (or longer if you feel you need it).

After connecting with the card daily, reflect on your experience.

Who Am I? Tarot Spread

This simple spread lays out who you are now, how you've evolved from the past, and exactly how to get to where you want to be. Use this spread any time you're feeling lost. It will help you feel grounded once again.

Shuffle the cards and cut the deck. Pull five cards in this spread format:

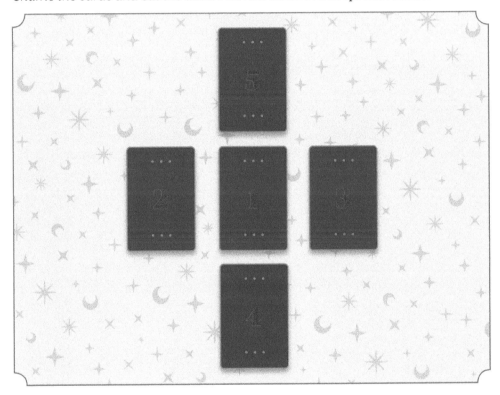

Card 1: *Who I am*

Card 2: *Who I was*

Card 3: *Who I want to be*

Card 4: *How to get there*

Card 5: *Advice*

CONTINUED >

*There are a few things to be aware of in this spread. First, take note of the suits involved and how they interact with each other. For example, if **Card 2** includes Cups and **Card 1** shows Pentacles, this shows a level of maturity gained around being too sensitive. What suits are involved in your spread?*

---

*Next, take note of any court cards. What are they and where do they land? Court cards detail how mature you are with respect to where the card lands in the spread. For example, seeing a Page of Wands as **Card 1** and a Queen of Swords as **Card 3** would indicate that you may have issues with believing that you can accomplish your goals and perhaps that you have issues with follow-through or creating actionable plans for those goals.*

---

*Next, focus on **Card 5**. What does the advice card tell you about a practical next step? The suit of **Card 5** will give you practical advice around what kind of next steps to take. Wands would indicate a need to make better plans, Cups would indicate being true to your passions, Swords suggest taking actionable movement, and Pentacles suggest finding balance.*

Major Arcana "Progress Pull"

This exercise uses the "hero's journey" theory of the Major Arcana as a way to identify exactly where you land in respect to multiple areas of your life. See page 7 for an overview of this component of the Major Arcana.

Take out the twenty-two cards of the Major Arcana. Shuffle and pull one card for each of the following categories. Once you pull a card, write it down below, then put it back so the next category is shuffled with all twenty-two cards.

Spiritual journey: _____

Love journey: _____

Career journey: _____

Money journey: _____

Family journey: _____

Health journey: _____

Are there a few coincidences or similarities that stand out?

_____

_____

_____

_____

Which journeys are at the beginning of their cycle? Which ones are at the end?

_____

_____

_____

_____

Draw Your Present

This is a fun one. Did you know you can use tarot without actually using a tarot deck? As part of the "where you are now" discussion, this exercise asks you to take note of your immediate surroundings and find symbolism in them.

First, sit in a comfortable space in a room that you're very familiar with. Look around. What do you see? Draw the major symbols that you see—not necessarily the exact surroundings. For example, right now, I would probably draw three dogs, a cozy couch, and my long, viny hanging plant.

After you're finished, list out the motifs that you drew. In my case, this would be dogs, a couch, and a plant.

Next, ask yourself, "What does this scene mean to me? How does it shape me or what does it remind me of?" In my case, I would say: peace, quiet, and the value of serenity.

What tarot cards come to mind when you think about the above words?

Use these cards as a comfort when you feel overwhelmed. They can serve as a helpful reminder when you feel that you are drifting from where you want to go.

Sibling Cards

There are a few pairs of tarot cards that match another card in the deck very closely in meaning. For instance, both The Empress and the Nine of Pentacles represent self-respect and values. I might also pair the Two of Cups and The Lovers as symbols of love or relationships. I like to think of these pairs as sibling cards because one of the cards typically represents more maturity than the other. In the case of the Two of Cups/Lovers dynamic, The Lovers might be the younger sibling, as it represents fleeting and immature partnerships. The older sibling, the Two of Cups, indicates long-lasting love.

In this exercise, we'll use sibling cards to represent where you are now in relation to where you want to be. This will not only challenge your knowledge of the cards but also give you a better understanding of exactly what the discrepancy is between now and later.

First, think of a topic: love, career, family, self, spirituality, etc.

Next, shuffle the deck and pull one card. Identify that card here:

What card would you appropriate as the sibling card?

Choose a maturity level for the card you pulled:

THE YOUNGER SIBLING   THE OLDER SIBLING

Based on the above, what do you think you need to work on in order to get to where you want to be in the future? For example, if you chose the older sibling first, perhaps you need to lighten up a bit when exploring the next steps of your life.

Reading About Items and Favorites

Our most prized personal possessions can tell us a lot about who we are now. In this exercise, I'm going to ask you to name five defining items or possessions in your life that, for you, truly make life worth living. My list would include my dog, my horse, my mattress, my stand mixer, and my insulated winter boots.

List your five favorite possessions here:

_____

_____

_____

_____

_____

Now pull a card for each possession, asking why the item is so important to you. Write the name of each card:

Possession 1 card: _____

Possession 2 card: _____

Possession 3 card: _____

Possession 4 card: _____

Possession 5 card: _____

Next, assign a keyword based on the cards you pulled and their relation to the possession. For example, for my possession "mattress," I might put "peace" because I drew the Four of Swords, telling me my mattress gives me the ability to completely disconnect from the world.

Possession 1 keyword: _____

Possession 2 keyword: _____

Possession 3 keyword: _____

Possession 4 keyword: _____

Possession 5 keyword: _____

Finish the sentence below to close the exercise:

Most important to me right now is _____ ,

_____ , _____ ,

_____ , *and* _____ .

Dream Life Association Cards

There are many ways to practice working with your tarot deck, but I recommend making a personal association with each card. In doing this, you establish a very direct message for yourself. Whenever that card appears in the future, you automatically know what the message is. This exercise asks you to make associations between cards and your perfect life. You will write out how you want your life to look and pull association cards for each area.

First, answer the following questions. Be big, be bold, and go into minute detail about what you want. The universe is more giving to those who have a clear understanding of what they're asking for.

What does your dream life look like regarding:

Love?

_____

_____

_____

Career?

_____

_____

_____

Money?

_____

_____

_____

Family?

_____

_____

_____

_____

Spirituality?

_____

_____

_____

_____

Now that you have an idea of what you want, let's pull an association card for each topic. You will want to make the right associations, so be intentional with each pull. Write the names of the cards down.

Love: _____

Career: _____

Money: _____

Family: _____

Spirituality: _____

Strengths + Weaknesses Tarot Spread

We all have our strengths and points of weakness. This exercise is simply meant to explore who you are as a person. Tuning into your strengths and weaknesses can allow you to take action and progress from where you are right now. It can also show you where pitfalls might arise.

Pull five cards for "strengths" and five cards for "weaknesses."

STRENGTHS   WEAKNESSES

_____   _____

_____   _____

_____   _____

_____   _____

_____   _____

These ten cards are considered part of your core personality.

What's your favorite strength card? What does it mean to you? This card can be referred back to whenever you're feeling uncertain about yourself.

What's your least favorite weakness card? What does it say about how you handle conflict?

What's your least favorite strength card? Where do you find weakness here?

What's your favorite weakness card? Where do you find strength here?

Gratitude List

If we aren't grateful for what we have now, we won't be gifted anything else later. Energy works the same way with tarot: It will only work for you if you are grateful for the messages that it brings you.

The law of attraction states that whatever we think about, we bring about. But gratitude only works if you *feel* what you're grateful for. This exercise focuses on why you're grateful for certain things, which can help you get into that feeling zone and more easily attract what you want.

First, write down five things you're grateful for. Be very specific. For example, instead of writing "cooking," you might write, "Being able to create what I want all the time in the kitchen."

1. _____

2. _____

3. _____

4. _____

5. _____

Next, let's pull a card for each one. Ask the cards to indicate why you're grateful for each item. Using the cards, identify the "why."

Gratitude Card 1: _____

The "Why": _____

Gratitude Card 2: _____

The "Why": _____

Gratitude Card 3: _____

The "Why": _____

CONTINUED >

Gratitude Card 4: _____

The "Why": _____

Gratitude Card 5: _____

The "Why": _____

Spend some time looking at your gratitude cards, feeling the gratitude well up inside you. Do this for one minute a day, every day, and you'll start to attract the things that you want.

KEY TAKEAWAYS

The exercises in this chapter should give you a better sense of not only where you want to go, but how you can best go about getting there. This section includes ways to recognize both personal strengths and weaknesses in a constructive way that guides you in the right direction for accomplishing your goals.

As human beings, intuition is a real thing. We have access to all the information we need to get where we want to go. We know how to move through a plan and accomplish our dreams; this is something we are already gifted with. The only thing we need is the key to unlock that information. That's what tarot does for us.

- Tarot helps you unlock knowledge that you already have and follow your intuition.

- Gratitude is the key to getting what you want.

- You can use the "hero's journey," sibling cards, and other elements of tarot to help you form plans and guide you toward what to do next.

- Don't be afraid to dream big. The more specific you are about your dreams, the better.

CHAPTER 5

MENTAL AND EMOTIONAL WELL-BEING

This chapter covers mental well-being (the relationship you have with your personal mindset) and emotional well-being (the relationship you have with your feelings). Both of these categories can be hard for some people to get in touch with—especially if you don't consider yourself a touchy-feely kind of person. Tarot helps rationalize these categories so that even the most stoic person can engage with their mental and emotional health.

The mental well-being exercises in this section will challenge you to ask yourself whether your mindset is healthy. Are you thinking positively? Do you generally feel you can think clearly? In what way does negative self-talk limit you?

The emotional well-being exercises will challenge you to ask yourself whether your emotions are fully balanced. Do you feel steady? Does your heart outweigh your head? Can you use your feelings to find clarity?

We all unknowingly carry mental and emotional imbalances, which can easily hinder our success and block our intuition. Using tarot as a guide, this section provides exercises to help level out these imbalances.

Well-Being Quiz

This quiz is a starting point to help you identify your current mental and emotional health.

Circle the numbers in response to each prompt, with 1 symbolizing strongly disagree and 10 symbolizing strongly agree.

1. *I am calm right now.*

   1   2   3   4   5   6   7   8   9   10

2. *I have great relationships with friends.*

   1   2   3   4   5   6   7   8   9   10

3. *I am happy with my body.*

   1   2   3   4   5   6   7   8   9   10

4. *I am happy with myself.*

   1   2   3   4   5   6   7   8   9   10

5. *I am proud of myself.*

   1   2   3   4   5   6   7   8   9   10

6. *I never self-criticize.*

   1   2   3   4   5   6   7   8   9   10

7. *I feel confident.*

   1   2   3   4   5   6   7   8   9   10

Now add up your numbers: _____

Below 10: *Your well-being needs much more attention*

10 to 20: *You're surviving, but you could use more self-love and personal TLC.*

Above 20: *Your well-being is on its way to success. Keep up the good work.*

Say Goodbye to Negative Self-Talk

When we tell ourselves that we aren't good enough, it's only a matter of time before we actually start to believe it. In this exercise, you'll be challenged to face the negative things that you most frequently tell yourself and use tarot to uncover how to rewire this thinking.

Shuffle the deck and pull five cards. Do so with the intention of drawing out the five most negative things you repeat to yourself. Write the names of the cards down here and identify what the negative mindset is. For instance, if I chose The Empress, I might write down that I tell myself I'm not as beautiful as others.

NEGATIVE CARD

WHAT I TELL MYSELF

_____   _____

_____   _____

_____   _____

_____   _____

Next, pull a new mindset card for each negative card. This will identify how to rewire the negative mindset with something more positive. For example, if after pulling The Empress, I pull The Star, it might indicate that I need to consider the fact that we are all unique and I should be proud of and celebrate my unique qualities.

NEGATIVE CARD   POSITIVE CARD   NEW MINDSET

_____   _____   _____

_____   _____   _____

_____   _____   _____

_____   _____   _____

How Am I Feeling?

This exercise seems simple, but it can be immensely helpful to gauge where your mindset and emotions are at any given time. This exercise makes use of what I like to call flier cards. Flier cards seem to jump out of the deck as you shuffle them. Whenever this happens, I always consider it very important. It's like the cards are literally popping out to send you a message.

As you shuffle, ask the cards, "How am I feeling?" Continue shuffling while repeating this question until a card leaps or flies out of the deck. Write that card down here:

Next, identify what this card means to you today. Is it happy or sad? Is it hopeful? Attempt to figure out what kind of access this card grants you into your emotions today and go from there. Write down your reflections here:

Songs + Tarot

Learning tarot involves using a lot of associations. We get good at reading cards when we start making associations with each card, because when the card comes up, it's an immediate connection. Songs are the same way. Do you have certain songs in your mental playlist that take you back years—maybe even *decades*—when you hear them? This exercise will help you make quicker associations with positive tarot cards when you're feeling down.

Think of a song that really pumps you up. This is an upbeat and happy-go-lucky song that always gets you feeling excited and ready for the day. Write the name of that song here:

Now put on headphones and play that song. As you listen and groove, shuffle the deck and ask it to give you three tarot cards that represent this song. Draw them and write them down:

Now you've associated your "pump up" song with your "pump up" tarot cards. The next time you feel down, try pulling out one of these cards and holding it in your hands. Stare at it, feel it, and let the positive vibes lift you up.

Mind, Body, Soul Tarot Spread

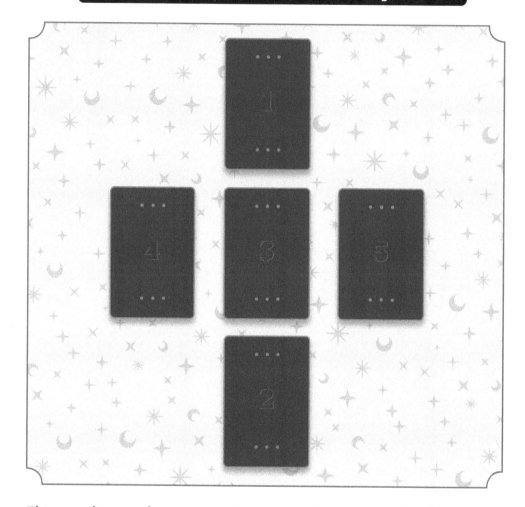

This spread is great for moments when you feel that your overall well-being is unbalanced. Maybe you think something feels off, but you just can't figure out how or why. Maybe you know that attention to your mindset could use some work, but you don't know where to start. This tarot spread helps you decipher exactly where the imbalance is and how to get started on next steps.

I've set up the layout so that mind, body, and soul are all reflected in a visual way. The "mind" card is at the very top, like a head, the "body" card is at the bottom, and the "soul" card in the middle.

Pull this spread:

Card 1: *Mind*

Card 2: *Body*

Card 3: *Soul*

Card 4: *Am I balanced?*

Card 5: *How to bring myself into balance*

Reflect on what part of you requires balance.

_____   _____

_____   _____

_____   _____

_____   _____

Name a few activities that would enable more balance according to the cards you pulled. For example, if you pulled a Five of Swords for **Card 2** *(Body), perhaps this means you need to find a way to reconnect with your body, such as yoga or meditation.*

_____   _____

_____   _____

_____   _____

_____   _____

Find the Theme

Tarot is a helpful tool when we need to understand why we feel a certain way. On a day when you feel less upbeat or happy, use this exercise to determine the root cause of the unhappiness.

Pick out three tarot cards that describe how you feel today. Write them out here:

Next, let's try to find similarities among all three cards. Look for repetition in any way you can. These will be your clues. For example, are there any repeating suits? Are there more feminine energies as opposed to masculine? Are the cards inherently sad? List all the similarities and ideas as to why they may appear together.

Given all the similarities, let's ask the cards to give us an all-encompassing card for the three cards above. This card will act as the main theme that ties our three emotions together. Shuffle, draw, and write down the card you get here:

Given the card above, what is the theme here? What is the root cause of your unhappiness today?

Emotion-Processor Exercise

You can do this any time you come across emotions that you don't understand. This exercise helps identify the emotion, process it, and come to an understanding of it.

First, pull a card that best describes this emotion. This card will identify exactly what the emotion is. Write the name of the card: _____

Next, write down one way you would explain this card to a friend:

Next, pick a "processor" card. This card will identify how to process the emotion. Write the name of the card: _____

How does this card tell you to process your emotion? In what way does it ask you to see it differently? From there, write down what this means to you:

Finally, pick an "actionable" card. This card will identify what to do next. Write the name of the card: _____

Next, write three actions you could take based on this card:

Doodle-Your-Own Tarot Card

Sometimes, the most rejuvenating thing we can do for ourselves is to engage in an art project that allows us to open our minds, touch our soul, and have some fun. This exercise asks you to create your own tarot card based on your favorite symbols and images. Let's create a tarot card that means "blissful happiness" for you.

First, draw your favorite landscape scene (e.g., ocean, mountains, countryside). This will serve as the background for your tarot card.

Next, doodle a couple of symbols and shapes that you really enjoy (e.g., triangles, pentacles, Venus glyph):

Then draw a few of your favorite things (e.g., tea, cats, mountains):

Finally, draw a few or all of those things together in this card:

Healthy + Unhealthy Cards

This exercise asks you to go through the entire tarot deck and pick out cards that represent a "healthy" you and other cards that indicate an "unhealthy" you. We will break things down into five different categories: self-talk, drive and motivation, mood and perspective, body and self-image, and, finally, spirituality.

Pick five cards that best resemble HEALTHY representations for each of these five categories:

SELF-TALK	DRIVE + MOTIVATION	MOOD + PERSPECTIVE	BODY + SELF-IMAGE	SPIRITUALITY

Next, pick five cards that best resemble UNHEALTHY representations of these five categories:

SELF-TALK	DRIVE + MOTIVATION	MOOD + PERSPECTIVE	BODY + SELF-IMAGE	SPIRITUALITY

What themes appear in the healthy cards compared to the unhealthy cards? Are there links between the two? Are there similarities or differences?

KEY TAKEAWAYS

When our mental and emotional well-being is in sync, we can better connect with who we are and what our intuition is telling us. More than that, when our minds and emotions are balanced, we become more balanced as people. When they say that you have to work from within, they really mean it.

The exercises in this section use tarot to explore your mental and emotional states. If you feel off-kilter or unbalanced, you can use tarot to point you in the right direction and bring you closer to a more balanced inner self.

◆ The key to a balanced inner self is to consider how you think about things (mental health) and process emotions (emotional health).

◆ When our well-being is blocked or unbalanced, we can struggle to achieve success and connect with our intuition.

◆ Tarot can provide a helpful perspective when we know something feels off, but we can't quite identify it.

◆ Tarot provides an accessible way to get in touch with mental and emotional well-being, even if you're not an emotional person.

CHAPTER 6

SOCIAL LIFE AND COMMUNITY

In this chapter, we'll uncover how you approach the outside world. It's a natural human tendency to try and view ourselves from the perspective of the world around us. But are you someone who relies heavily on the assurance of others? Do you lose your identity in the crowd if you stick with certain people for too long? How do you deal with the word *community*? Do you prefer being alone or do you find community with other people?

Because we live in a relational world, social and community obstacles are everywhere. Issues like family pressure, ethics, social skills, societal obligations, and hierarchical expectations can pop up in many areas of our lives. How you approach these influences may be completely different from how someone else might. This section of the book is meant to help you understand and overcome those obstacles.

The exercises in this section of the workbook will bring to light the dichotomy between "the individual" and "the other" (other people, the outside world, etc.). The aim of this section is to challenge you to find personal acceptance and identity without the influence of others. These exercises can help you find *you* again, without the outside noise.

Mirror Tarot Spread

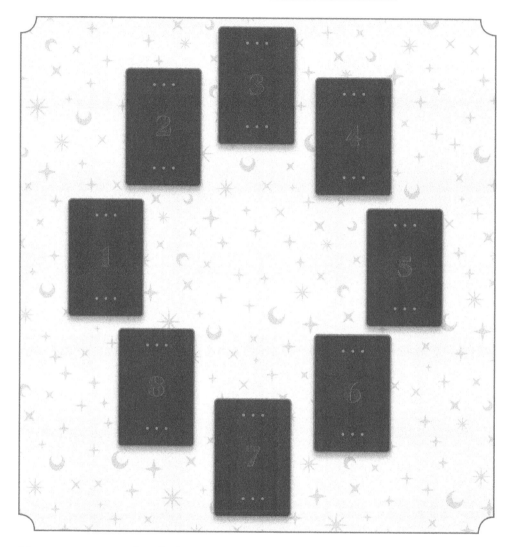

Have you ever wondered what other people see in you? While we have our own view of who we are in this world, it's often a one-sided mindset. After all, regardless of how hard we try to understand another person's perspective, we can really only see through one lens: our own. Tarot allows you to consider new perspectives, ones that you wouldn't have the ability to make sense of without this outlet.

This tarot spread helps you identify the views of others. The answers you glean from this spread may surprise you. They can also help you understand and deepen your relationships. I made the layout of the spread an oval to mimic the shape of a mirror.

Shuffle the cards and pull this spread to answer the following questions:

1. *How do I see myself?*

2. *How do my romantic partners see me?*

3. *How do my friends see me?*

4. *How does my family see me?*

5. *How do my coworkers see me?*

6. *How does my boss see me?*

7. *How does this tarot deck see me?*

8. *Is there a connection or theme?*

Side note: If you'd like to know about a specific person (say, your mother), you can always swap one of the questions out or add another one.

After you pull the spread, write down which answers surprised you the most and why.

Finding Your Happy Place

Our surroundings can put us at ease or create even more anxiety. Because of this, it's so important to find our literal happy place. This exercise uses tarot to help you narrow down where that happy environment is for you.

First, pick five different environments to try. Try to include a wide variety of locations, such as the office, the beach, or on the porch.

Environment 1: _____

Environment 2: _____

Environment 3: _____

Environment 4: _____

Environment 5: _____

Now, take your deck to each of the environments. Sit cross-legged on the ground. Start shuffling your tarot deck, close your eyes, take a deep breath, and pull one card.

As you do this, note your surroundings and how the process feels. Are you comfortable? Distracted? Frazzled? Take note of the card you pulled. Does it resemble peace?

Now rank your comfort level from 1 to 10, with 1 being the lowest.

Environment 1: _____

1   2   3   4   5   6   7   8   9   10

Environment 2: _____

1   2   3   4   5   6   7   8   9   10

Environment 3: _____

   1   2   3   4   5   6   7   8   9   10

Environment 4: _____

   1   2   3   4   5   6   7   8   9   10

Environment 5: _____

   1   2   3   4   5   6   7   8   9   10

Social Personality Court Card Quiz

This exercise aims to identify how social you are, what kind of social skills you naturally possess, and whether you enjoy solitude or group settings.

Circle the answers that best represent you.

1. *On Friday night, you can find me . . .*

    a. *Finishing off my work*

    b. *Cooking a great meal*

    c. *Calling my besties for wine and cheese*

    d. *Starting a party*

2. *Do you use social media?*

    a. *Hardly or never*

    b. *For business and sometimes for personal*

    c. *All the time—selfies and friends*

    d. *I keep forgetting to create an account*

3. *Which word best describes you?*

    a. *Willful*

    b. *Nurturing*

    c. *Independent*

    d. *Optimistic*

4. *How many best friends do you have?*

    a. *One or two*

    b. *Three to five*

    c. *Six to nine*

    d. *More than ten*

5. *Which do you prefer?*

    a. *Alone time*

    b. *"Me" time*

    c. *Time with friends*

    d. *Party time*

Mostly As: *King*

Mostly Bs: *Queen*

Mostly Cs: *Page*

Mostly Ds: *Knight*

Using your result from this quiz, apply the court card to the suit you chose in the "Which Suit Am I? Quiz" on page 54 in chapter 3. Write down your court card:

Family Pressure Exercise

Regardless of our age, many of us struggle to get along with our parents. This exercise is designed to help you understand your parents or parental figures. When you know someone better, you can better relate to them.

First, pull out the court card section of the deck. This should include twelve cards. Shuffle this small section.

Pull cards to represent up to two parental figures. Write them down:

PARENT 1   PARENT 2

_____   _____

If you have pulled two cards, what do you see in this pair? Looking at them together, would you assume that they work well together? Where are the differences?

_____

_____

_____

_____

Now look at each card through the lens of "parenting style." How do the cards represent each person's role as a parent?

_____

_____

_____

_____

What would you guess is the love language of each court card? Take note of the suits and the maturity level of each court card. For example, a Queen of Wands might enjoy words of affirmation, whereas the Knight of Pentacles may enjoy gift-giving.

PARENT 1   PARENT 2

_____   _____

How can you incorporate this love language in your interaction with each parent?

_____

_____

_____

_____

_____

_____

_____

_____

_____

_____

_____

_____

_____

Society + Me Coloring Exercise

Today's world presents so many social challenges on a national and international scale. It can be difficult to separate yourself as an individual from the community around you.

In the tarot deck, the card Justice directly reflects on this topic. It's about ethics, morals, and doing the right thing according to society's needs. This card often represents a "head versus heart" decision, where someone may be struggling to decipher where they land within the social obligations of the greater community.

To meditate on the concept of society, color in Justice. Take note of the symbols you see in this card, what colors you choose, and how Justice's facial expression makes you feel.

Next, pick out a card to represent "you" within society. This card will identify how you act within the confines of social structure. Are you inherently rebellious, or do you prefer to fit in with the crowd?

Shuffle the deck, ask this question, and use a flier card to find the answer. Write your card here:

How is this card connected to or different from Justice? What does that say about your connection to community?

JUSTICE

How I've Changed Tarot Spread

Tarot can help us home in on our true selves and examine where we came from. This exercise is meant to help you locate who you are and what your story is as it relates to the world around you. How have you developed as a function of your environment (friends, family, location, etc.)?

This spread is set up with two columns. This layout will help you make connections easily between the "self" and the "surroundings."

Shuffle and draw cards for this tarot spread:

1. *Past self*

2. *Current self*

3. *Future self*

4. *Past surroundings*

5. *Current surroundings*

6. *Future surroundings*

Write your findings:

1. _____

2. _____

3. _____

4. _____

5. _____

6. _____

Look at the cards from the perspective of the time periods. In your past, what was your environment like? How did that shape your identity?

_____

_____

How does your current environment relate to your identity?

_____

_____

What about your future environment and future self? What are some possible changes that you see taking place here (good or bad)?

_____

_____

_____

_____

_____

Personal Community: Your Pack

This is a fun exercise because it centers on your pack: the people you love and surround yourself with. What kind of community do you choose to create for yourself? Within this private circle, we might see friends, family members, lovers, or acquaintances.

The goal of this exercise is to find a common thread between all these people you hold dear. Uncover the qualities they possess that are attractive to you. Ultimately, it asks the question, why them?

Let's bring in a wide range of people. First, name two best friends:

1. _____

2. _____

Now, name a favorite family member:

3. _____

Next, name a favorite coworker:

4. _____

Finally, name the romantic partner you've loved the most (or pick a nonromantic love):

5. _____

Go through the deck and select a signifier tarot card for each person:

1. _____

2. _____

3. _____

4. _____

5. _____

Look at these five tarot cards together. What do they have in common? Would you consider them fun or serious? Do they have common suits?

_____

_____

_____

_____

_____

Write a few adjectives to describe the people in your pack:

_____   _____

_____   _____

_____   _____

_____   _____

_____   _____

_____   _____

_____   _____

Group Tarot

Grab your mom, grab a friend, grab your cat—it doesn't matter. This exercise is all about reading tarot in front of others. We could all use a little practice doing live readings for others.

If you're already a pro at live readings, use this exercise to try out a spread you're not familiar with.

First, choose someone to read for. If you're shy or live alone, it's totally fine to read in front of a pet. Write down the individual you've chosen: _____

Pull three cards for this individual. Before you start reading, remember this:

◆ *Don't rush.*

◆ *Read the cards one by one so you don't get overwhelmed.*

◆ *Try not to read into your audience's facial expressions.*

After you finish your reading, rate your confidence level doing this activity:

1   2   3   4   5   6   7   8   9   10

If your confidence level is below a 5, you might want to practice this activity again. If it is above a 5, you might want to try a harder subject next time. Test yourself.

Reflect on your confidence level and overall experience:

_____

_____

_____

_____

_____

_____

_____

Outer Community: Your World

It's important to recognize what community means to you, and how much of it you need in your life. Do you relate to others on a macro or a micro level? For example, people who enjoy having a wide net of acquaintances may relate to others on a macro level, while people who prefer to socialize with a select few best friends might relate to others on a micro level. This differentiates the humanitarians from the individualists. To be clear: It doesn't matter which one you are, as both are valid ways of living. The important part is recognizing what type of person you are so you can better analyze how you participate in the world around you.

First, take out the Major Arcana section of the tarot deck. Shuffle this section and ask the cards to show you just how involved you are in your outer community.

Pull a card and write it down: _____

This card shows your level of involvement in your community, depending on how far into the Major Arcana it is. For example, if you receive The Fool (0), you're an extreme individualist. If you pick Judgment (20), you're much more integrated in humanitarian efforts.

Circle one that best relates:

MACRO   MICRO

What kind of community do you need? Circle one:

GLOBAL   WIDE NET   PERSONAL

KEY TAKEAWAYS

This chapter included exercises to help you uncover who you are, what you stand for, and how you interact with others and the community around you. "The individual" versus "the other" can manifest in different ways for different people. For example, some might prefer to have a small group of friends whereas others may wish for many acquaintances around them. The exercises in this section of the workbook are designed to help you find a sense of individualism in a relational world. We can also use tarot to identify the various social pressures we face on a daily basis.

◆ We live in a relational world where our individualist perspective is at risk of being dimmed.

◆ The dynamic of "the individual" versus "the other" can be explored through many lenses.

◆ Humanitarians and individualists approach community differently.

◆ Social pressure is everywhere. Tarot is a key tool to help you navigate it.

CHAPTER 7

LOVE AND ROMANCE

Love truly makes the world go round. Love is part of human nature, and we could all use a little more of it. Unfortunately, love isn't always easy. It can be tiresome, confusing, and gut-wrenching. Using tarot can reveal secrets about love that you have yet to uncover on your own. Tarot is an ideal tool for analyzing how past and present love experiences have shaped you. It's also excellent for revealing the perspectives of others, particularly a potential love interest or partner.

In this section, we'll use tarot to dive into every facet of love. These exercises will explore how you approach love, what your past is like, what kind of love patterns you've fallen into, who your "type" is, how to use tarot for timing, and how to find love if you haven't already. If you have developed a negative relationship with love, this section will help you reconfigure your perception of what love is. Or if you have an optimistic view of love, this section aims to help bring more of it into your life.

In this chapter in particular, feel free to adjust these exercises to your specific situation. Whether you have one partner, multiple partners, aromantic or asexual relationships, or any other type of relationship, you can find ways to apply the lessons of each exercise. Love is always within reach.

What Does "Love" Mean to You?

Love is such a fluid and unique concept. Everyone has a different interpretation. What one person considers to be expressing love is quite different from the next. This exercise asks you to define what love means to you so that you're able to assess your needs early on in a relationship.

Go through the tarot deck and select five cards that scream "love" to you. Write them down here:

_____

_____

_____

_____

Now let's rank them. Order them from most important to least important to you:

1. _____

2. _____

3. _____

4. _____

5. _____

Look at the top two cards. How do they describe what love means to you? What are key pillars for you in partnership? For example, if The Lovers is placed first, perhaps that means you need lust above all else. If the Ten of Pentacles is first, perhaps this means you need stability and consistency.

    Write down how your top two love cards embody your version of love:

_____

_____

_____

Me vs. "Relationship Me"

Have you ever heard—from friends or family—that you change once you get into a relationship? In this exercise, we'll uncover just how healthy your approach to relationships is.

Let's first pull a card that describes you (who you are and what you stand for). Name your **"me" card** *here and write about how it describes you:*

_____

_____

Now pull a card that describes how you are in a relationship (how you approach love, yourself, and your partner). Name your **"relationship me" card** *here:*

_____

How does the "relationship me" card differ from the "me" card?

_____

_____

If the "me" card could speak to the "relationship me" card, what kind of advice do you think it would give?

_____

_____

Based on this information, write down some behaviors to be mindful of next time you're in a relationship:

1. _____

2. _____

3. _____

Relationship Analysis Tarot Spread

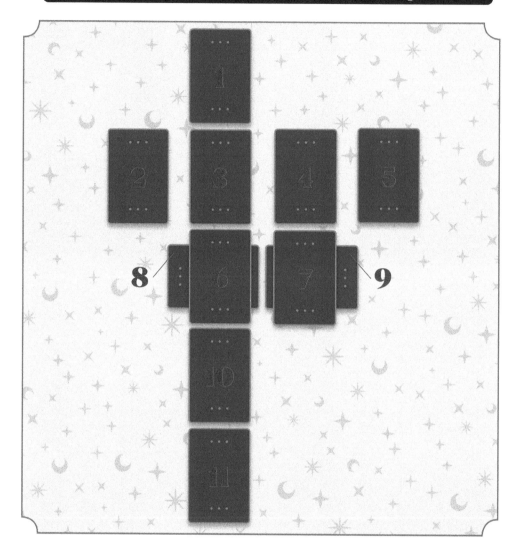

Do you want to know whether you and your partner are meant to be together? This tarot spread uncovers the strengths in your partnership as well as areas where you might need to sprinkle in a little TLC.

This spread is configured with two separate columns, allowing an easy visual comparison of "you" vs. "me" in the partnership. In order to identify challenges, we need to view the disparities side by side.

Pull the cards:

Card 1: *The relationship as it stands*

Card 2: *Me in this relationship*

Card 3: *My partner in this relationship*

Card 4: *One thing I love about my partner*

Card 5: *One thing my partner loves about me*

Card 6: *What I'm missing*

Card 7: *What my partner is missing*

Card 8: *How I see the future of the relationship*

Card 9: *How my partner sees the future of the relationship*

Card 10: *Will this relationship be successful?*

Card 11: *Advice*

Describe your reflections. Take note of the following considerations:

◆ *What kind of "card maturity" does **Card 1** have? Does it fall late in the Major Arcana? Did you pull a Knight as opposed to a King?*

◆ *What is the power dynamic between **Card 2** (me) and **Card 3** (partner)?*

◆ *Is **Card 6** something you've thought of before?*

◆ *How does **Card 11** communicate with **Card 10**?*

Find Me Love Tarot Spread

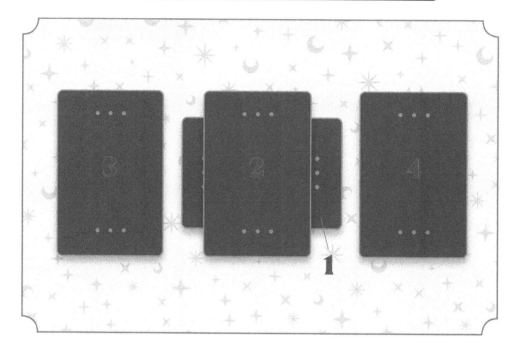

This exercise is for anyone looking for love. I adore this small spread because it homes in on how your past relationship history affects your present love life. I truly believe that the partnerships of our past (whether good or bad) have a dramatic effect on how we view love now.

This four-card tarot spread is easy to grasp and gets straight to the point. I've added a physical element where one card actually covers the other in order, representing a "blockage" in love.

Shuffle and draw cards for this spread:

1. *Current relationship with love*

2. *Key challenges blocking you from love*

3. *Past issues that may be affecting present love life*

4. *Advice*

Write them out here:

Card 1: _____

Card 2: _____

Card 3: _____

Card 4: _____

*How is your current relationship with love (**Card 1**)? Is it healthy? Is it engaging?*

_____

_____

_____

_____

_____

_____

_____

*How does **Card 2** (challenge) interact with **Card 3** (the past)? Is **Card 2** in any way a manifestation of **Card 3**?*

_____

_____

_____

_____

_____

_____

_____

_____

_____

A Letter to Your Ex

Exes can be tough to let go of, especially if you've been through an intense or serious relationship. They say that writing letters and burning them can be healing, allowing you to release past concerns into the ash. This exercise is based on that idea and aims to help you find closure from the past in a safe and protected way.

First, divide up your tarot deck. Separate the cards into three piles: Major Arcana, court cards, and the rest of the Minor Arcana.

These piles will help you write a letter to your ex. Drawing from the pile that matches the category listed in the brackets below, pull a card to represent each blank. Write down the name of the card or what you associate with it.

Dear _____ [court card],

Our relationship was _____ [Minor Arcana card], but also _____ [Minor Arcana card]. The worst part about it is that I'm still carrying around _____ [Minor Arcana card] emotional wounds from it. You left me feeling _____ [Minor Arcana card]. But you know what? I've come to terms with the fact that we are no longer together. Our relationship helped me to prepare for _____ [Major Arcana card]. In fact, I'm more ready for true love because this relationship helped me learn _____ [Minor Arcana card].

Thank you for teaching me so much about what I need in love.

Sincerely, your ex,

_____ [court card]

Love + Timing

I get the question, "When will I find love?" all the time. As much as I want to give a straightforward answer, it's not always that simple. Whenever this happens, I tend to break the question up into parts. For example, the original question might be broken up into: What will my love life look like in one month? Six months? Twelve months? That way, tarot can answer specific timeline questions as opposed to a generalized one.

That said, in a quick pinch the tarot suits are a good indicator of time. If you're wondering about when something will happen, such as when someone will propose, use this guide:

♦ Wands (fire element): burns quickly—i.e., days

♦ Swords (air element): flows "logically" or as expected—i.e., weeks

♦ Cups (water element): ebbs and flows—i.e., months

♦ Pentacles (earth element): grows slowly—i.e., years or many months

Let's try it out. What's your "when" question?

Shuffle and pull one card. What card did you choose?

What's your speculated time frame?

Different-Deck "Lovers"

Every tarot deck is different from the next. While the cards share the same general meanings from deck to deck, the creative license each deck artist uses can display concepts in a new light. By comparing three love-related cards from different decks, this exercise offers a new way to approach love.

Take out three different tarot decks. (If you don't have three tarot decks, look up two others online.) Name the decks here:

_____

_____

_____

Now pull The Lovers card out from each of the three decks. Lay all three cards out side by side. What are some similarities and differences you can see in the cards?

SIMILARITIES   DIFFERENCES

_____   _____

_____   _____

_____   _____

_____   _____

What does each card say about love? How does each card represent love? Does it feel safe? Does it feel vulnerable? Does it feel terrifying?

Card 1: _____

Card 2: _____

Card 3: _____

Finally, identify which card you most resonate with: _____

Explain why:

_____

_____

_____

_____

_____

_____

_____

_____

_____

_____

_____

_____

_____

_____

_____

_____

_____

_____

_____

_____

Is My Relationship Healthy? Tarot Spread

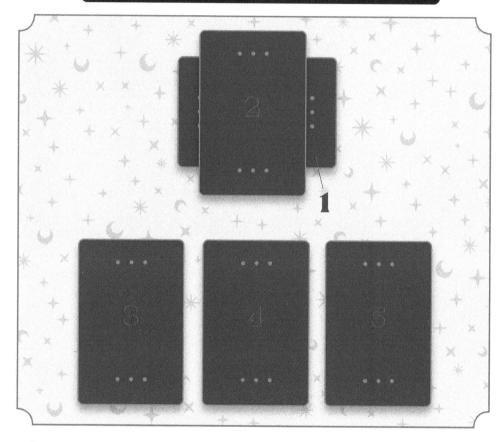

When we're on the inside attempting to look out, it can be difficult to see a situation with an objective point of view. When you're in love, the love goggles can easily become fogged. Suddenly we realize we've spent years with someone who doesn't make us happy.

This exercise aims to help you identify whether your relationship is healthy. It also helps you identify how the partnership is making you feel about yourself—a true indicator of either unhealthiness or happiness.

The layout for this spread is not complicated. We'll start with a signifier card at the top of the spread, and *Card 2* (what you're choosing not to see) is laid on top of it to "block" vision. Then all the messages are laid out below that.

Shuffle and draw cards for this tarot spread:

Card 1: *Who I am in this relationship*

Card 2: *What am I choosing not to see?*

Card 3: *What's healthy about my relationship?*

Card 4: *What's unhealthy about my relationship?*

Card 5: *Advice*

Note how you feel about **Card 1**. *Are you proud to represent this card? Is it descriptive of the person you want to be?*

Reflect on the rest of your findings here:

My Love Pattern Quiz

This exercise encourages you to identify how you approach love and, potentially, how that approach is unhealthy. More than this, it will help uncover what you need from a partner in order to feel safe and comfortable in a relationship.

First, pull a signifier card for each serious partner you've had. (No need to attempt to fill up all the blanks. Alternatively, if you have more than three, feel free to add them all.)

NAME: _____ CARD: _____

NAME: _____ CARD: _____

NAME: _____ CARD: _____

Now let's take a small quiz using the signifier cards. Circle the answers that apply.

Most of the signifier cards have . . .

MASCULINE ENERGY	FEMININE ENERGY
Anger	*Sadness*
Court cards	*Major Arcana*
Dramatic imagery	*Peaceful imagery*
Harmful energy	*Healthy energy*
Swords	*Cups*
Wands	*Pentacles*

Which column has more circled items?

LEFT   **RIGHT**

Given this information, review the harmful traits below. Circle any that stand out:

LEFT	RIGHT
Controlling	*Clingy*
Distant	*Overly helpful or perfectionistic*
Childish	*Unable to set boundaries*
Manipulative	*Unrealistic*

KEY TAKEAWAYS

Tarot is a handy tool for identifying who you are in love and how you tend to approach relationships. These exercises are designed to remind you that love is within your grasp, even if you've lost touch with your partner or lost hope that you will find someone. Tarot helps us step out of our one-dimensional mind or singular perspective and focus on something else, like the partner in front of us or the relationship as a whole. Doing so reveals strengths and weaknesses as well as the perspectives of others.

Using the various tarot exercises in this section, you may have redefined your perspective and relationship with romance so that you can more easily attract it for yourself. Ideally, you've found a new relationship with love (and with any partners).

◆ Tarot can help you reframe your relationship with love in a new light.

◆ Love is always within reach.

◆ Tarot can be used to find closure, uncover history, and identify relationship patterns.

◆ Even if you feel a lack of love, there are ways to help you bring more of it into your life.

CHAPTER 8

WORK AND PROSPERITY

Many of us tend to have a skewed perception of success, and one person's version of success doesn't necessarily match up with another's. It is easy to get caught in a career path or a vision of success that doesn't work for us as an individual. I believe that success is measured only by the willingness we have to dream bigger. This chapter will help you start thinking about what *you* want, as opposed to what you think you're supposed to want.

This section will allow you to dream big and expand your thinking around what you can accomplish. Most important, these exercises encourage you to be proud of what you've already accomplished in your lifetime. (I'm sure it's a lot more than you think.)

Tarot is helpful in uncovering work/life dynamics because it's an emotionally detached tool, which helps you get from A to Z without getting caught up in strong feelings. Using tarot as a guidance tool (and sometimes an actual how-to guide), this section will help you redefine what prosperity means to you. You will explore big-picture career topics like how to find your passion, as well as methods for navigating common work situations, like handling a difficult boss or making big career decisions.

Find Your Passion Tarot Spread

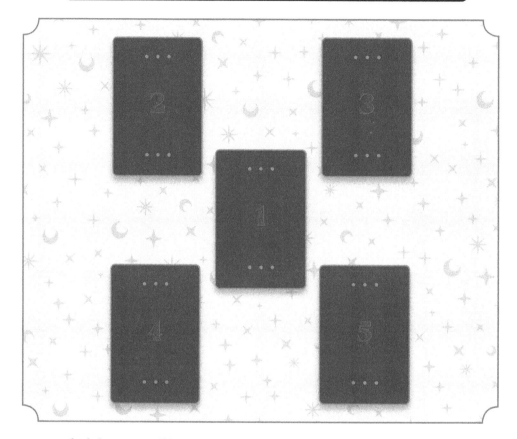

Do you feel that you still haven't found your true purpose in the career field? Has nothing quite sparked passion yet? This is a quick and easy tarot spread that will help you identify where your natural passions lie and what the best career would be for you.

Select signifier cards you associate with the following prompts:

1. *My deepest passion*

2. *My natural talents*

3. *My fears in exploring my passion*

4. *A potential career option (passion + talent)*

5. *Something I haven't considered*

Now write out the cards you picked:

Card 1: _____

Card 2: _____

Card 3: _____

Card 4: _____

Card 5: _____

Next, unravel the story behind those cards. How are **Card 1** *(passion) and* **Card 2** *(talents) similar? How are they different?*

_____

_____

Using just that information, what kind of career ideas can you come up with?

For example, if you received the Two of Cups (romantic relationships) for passion and The Magician (communications and plans) for talents, you might add "couple's therapist" as an option here.

_____

_____

Do any of those options above relate to **Card 4** *(potential career option)?*

_____

For **Card 3** *(fears), what is the fear and when have you experienced this fear before?*

_____

For **Card 5** *(something you haven't considered), how does it align with your fears—if at all?*

_____

Get Along with Your Boss

In this exercise, we'll focus on all of your boss's personality quirks and intricacies. This will help you maintain a natural and easygoing connection with them.

First, we'll go through the process of picking out your boss's signifier card—the one card in the deck that truly embodies their presence at the office.

List all the tarot cards that you might associate with your boss:

_____

_____

_____

Next, pull cards for each category related to your boss:

Their temperament at work: _____

Their relationship with you: _____

Their good traits: _____

Their not-so-good traits: _____

Their favorite thing to be praised about: _____

What they admire in an employee: _____

Do any of the cards in the first section overlap with the cards in the second section? Is there one card that you feel really embodies your boss at work? **Identify that card** *here as the signifier:*

_____

Now that you have your signifier, locate where you two connect ... and where you do not. Write down everything about the signifier card that resonates with you or that you disconnect from.

CONNECTIONS   DISCONNECTIONS

_____   _____

_____   _____

_____   _____

_____   _____

_____   _____

Looking at your lists, do you recognize any natural similarities or gaps between you and your boss? Using this information, write down how to best approach your boss at work. What can you do that would make them really enjoy you as an employee? What interests do you share? How can you find ways to connect?

_____

_____

_____

_____

_____

_____

_____

_____

_____

_____

_____

_____

Befriending Pride

All too often, we're bashful about proclaiming and acknowledging our accomplishments. Perhaps it's because we don't want to seem boastful or we don't believe we deserve the recognition. Whatever it may be, this exercise attempts to break down that self-limiting pattern. Reconnect with your self-worth and take pride in all that you do.

Shuffle the cards and pull three cards that signify the greatest, proudest moments in your career as a _____.

Write them down, one by one, and provide explanations for why you feel proud of this moment and what key takeaways you can recall when you're feeling low.

Proud Moment #1: _____

Why do you feel proud of this moment:

_____

_____

_____

Key takeaways:

◆ _____

◆ _____

◆ _____

Proud Moment #2: _____

Why do you feel proud of this moment:

_____

_____

_____

Key takeaways:

- _____
- _____
- _____

Proud Moment #3: _____

Why do you feel proud of this moment:

_____

_____

_____

Key takeaways:

- _____
- _____
- _____

Pros + Cons List

Are you considering quitting your job or embarking on a new career path? If you're planning for change or in the midst of it, you can use tarot to create a list of pros and cons. This can help you see the best decision more clearly so you feel confident moving forward.

First, identify what you're grappling with. What's the situation? What potential path are you hoping to focus on?

_____

_____

_____

Next, shuffle the cards and focus on one of the decisions. Pull cards for the pro column, then pull cards for the con column, and note each card on the chart.

PROS	CONS

Judging by the cards above, circle the category that has more influence or power:

PROS   CONS

Write down a "need to know" card from the opposite list here: _____

    For example, perhaps everything looks great in the "Pros" list, but the Seven of Swords (secrets) appears in the "Cons" list. This is definitely something to keep in mind as you move forward.

Reflect on the decision:

_____

_____

_____

_____

_____

_____

_____

_____

_____

_____

_____

_____

_____

_____

_____

_____

_____

Prosperity Tarot Spread

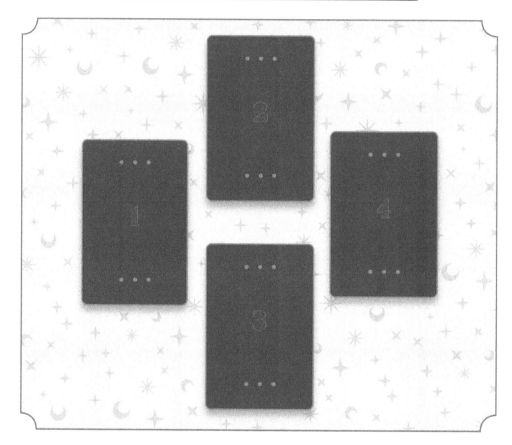

Are you ready to bring more fortune and success into your life? Perhaps you don't know where to start or how to accomplish this. This tarot spread aims to open your eyes to all the financial potential in front of you. It not only encourages motivation, but it also widens the scope of your current money dreams.

This is a four-card spread because the number four is symbolic of stability and prosperity. This tarot spread's layout is in the shape of a circle to represent continual, cyclical success.

Shuffle the cards and pull this spread:

1. *Your relationship with money*

2. *How it could improve*

3. *What you need to release to attract more money*

4. *A tip for financial abundance*

Based on this card, is your relationship with money positive and healthy? Does this card surprise you in any way?

_____

_____

_____

_____

How do you interpret **Card 3**? *What is it asking you to let go of? Does this relate to any mental blocks related to financial success?*

_____

_____

_____

_____

Reflect on the rest of your findings.

_____

_____

_____

_____

Color-Me-Money

This is a fun coloring exercise that asks you to connect deeply with one of the most abundant cards in the tarot deck: the Ace of Pentacles.

Pentacles represent material things like our home, career, finances, and family. Aces are all about new beginnings. So, the Ace of Pentacles reflects a time when new financial or career opportunities abound for us. Focusing on this abundant card can help you resonate more with the potential in front of you.

First, pull the Ace of Pentacles card from the deck. Look at the colors and imagery. Write down the symbols on the card that represent abundance.

Now, color in the card from start to finish. Put more emphasis on coloring in the symbols you mentioned.

After you finish coloring, you may want to hang your picture on the wall or keep it at your desk as a reminder of the abundance of potential that awaits you in the world.

ACE OF PENTACLES

Career Predictions

We all want to know what's going to happen in the future. This is especially true when we're searching for a job or starting a new career. I usually choose to stay away from tarot pulls that are meant to show the future, but future pulls can be really helpful for career advancement. These pulls are meant to give us a little heads-up about major changes.

In this exercise, we'll pull a few cards while focusing on certain periods of time.

Shuffle the cards and pull two cards for this question: What will likely happen in one month? Write them down here:

_____

_____

_____

Reflect on the prediction for the next month.

_____

_____

Now pull two cards for: What will likely happen in six months? Write them down here:

_____

_____

Reflect on the prediction for the next six months.

_____

_____

_____

Finally, pull two cards for: What will likely happen in one year? Write them down here:

_____

_____

Reflect on the prediction for a year from now.

_____

_____

_____

Using this information, circle your answers for the following questions:

Where do you see the biggest changes?

    1 MONTH   6 MONTHS   1 YEAR

What are you most excited about?

    1 MONTH   6 MONTHS   1 YEAR

What period of time will require a little extra care?

    1 MONTH   6 MONTHS   1 YEAR

Vision Board

A vision board is a visual collection of desires or dreams. Typically, this board is placed somewhere you can see it every day, as a way to keep your dreams in the forefront of your mind. Tarot cards are a great tool for quick-and-easy vision board creation. This exercise will use the cards to help you lock down your most idyllic career life.

First, grab your deck and shuffle the cards. As you shuffle, think about how ecstatic you would be with your career if you had everything you wanted. What would it feel like? What would that life look like? Consider these things in your head and shuffle until three cards fly out of the deck.

Write them down here:

_____

_____

_____

_____

How do these cards describe your best career life?

_____

_____

_____

_____

Now take the three cards and keep them in a special place where you can see them every day. You can choose to keep them at your desk or physically hang them on the wall. Attempt to meditate on the cards daily to manifest the dream career life that you desire.

Interview Prep

In this exercise, we'll use tarot as a career adviser to help you prepare for a job interview. Discover what kind of person will be interviewing you and how to get in their good graces. Tarot is exceptionally good at creating character profiles for individuals—even the ones you haven't met yet.

First, pull a signifier card for the person who will be interviewing you:

Now use adjectives to describe how this person might be in an office or interview setting. Are they forceful? Friendly? Optimistic? Stubborn?

Knowing the above, what do you think your approach should be to this kind of person? What kind of employee would they appreciate?

Finally, pull a few advice cards. These cards will tell you what qualities or strengths to highlight in your interview, strengths this particular interviewer will appreciate.

CONTINUED >

What do you make of the advice cards? What will you highlight about yourself in the interview?

_____

_____

_____

_____

KEY TAKEAWAYS

It's important to remember that success and prosperity look different for every individual. These exercises allow you to redefine what a successful work life looks like in your mind. More than that, this section aims to encourage you to dream bigger in the world of work and money.

The reason tarot is such a fabulous tool for defining and exploring career goals is because the cards can identify how to get from one place to the next. Using tarot to explore your past, present, and future can help widen the scope of your dreams.

- Prosperity looks different for every individual.

- Tarot is the best tool for career guidance because it does not take feelings into account.

- Reflecting on prosperity with tarot cards can help uncover motivation.

- Tarot can act as a "how-to" or step-by-step guide to achieve your career goals.

- You can use tarot to better understand work personalities, including current or future employers.

CHAPTER 9

OVERCOMING HARDSHIPS

Life is filled with beautiful, loving, and happy moments. But with sunshine, rain must also come. In contrast with our happiest moments, there are always times when we feel we cannot get any lower.

For these moments, it's so helpful to have tarot cards on hand. In addition to helping you reflect on situations with an objective perspective, they can help you find new insightful solutions. With these solutions, we're reminded that we cannot grow unless we face obstacles.

The exercises in this chapter are organized to broaden your perspective over time. We begin with exercises that will help you gain personal confidence and find inner strength. After that, the exercises move toward providing clarity. And finally, the last few exercises help you reflect on life's cycles of ups and downs and why they are necessary for your development. Overall, this section will help you identify and process hardships, and support you in finding positive opportunities for growth within them. It's all in an effort to start reconfiguring your mindset away from lack and toward gratitude for all experiences, both positive and negative.

Personal Strength Tarot Cards

This exercise uses tarot as a way to create positive vision boards or message boards. In this exercise, you will identify which cards you associate with personal strength, and why. Using this knowledge, you can start to figure out what your strengths are in times of privation.

First, select five cards in the tarot deck that you feel represent being STRONG.

Write the names of each card. Next to each name, write an adjective or two that you might use to describe a person who has this energy. For example, if you chose The Star, a brief description of someone like this might be "fearlessly optimistic."

Finally, after you choose your adjectives, explain why those adjectives are motivating for you. Why is being fearlessly optimistic a powerful trait or quality to have?

CARD	ADJECTIVES	REASON

CARD	ADJECTIVES	REASON

CARD	ADJECTIVES	REASON

CARD	ADJECTIVES	REASON

CONTINUED >

CARD	ADJECTIVES	REASON

Little do you know . . . the cards you chose are strengths that you value highly, but they are likely also strengths that you see in yourself (or that you are trying to improve in yourself).

Use these five cards as a reminder of your own personal strength, and the traits that will carry you through the toughest times. To commemorate them, find a way to frame or display these cards so you can see them daily.

Defining Emotions

When you're going through a tough time, it can be difficult to sort through your feelings. But how can you get yourself to a better place if you don't know what's wrong? This exercise aims to help you identify what the hardship is, as well as what emotions it's currently drawing out of you.

Choose a card that embodies your hardship: _____

Describe the situation and how it relates to the card: _____

_____

_____

Now pull three different cards to describe your emotions:

_____

_____

_____

Based on the cards above, how would you say this hardship is making you feel?

_____

_____

_____

_____

Not all hardships can be remedied all at once. Instead of attempting to fix the hardship, pull three cards to identify activities or actionable things you can do to counter these feelings (as you're working to fix the hardship):

_____

_____

_____

Harsh Truth Tarot Spread

Perhaps you'd like to ask a tougher question regarding your hardship, one you almost can't bear to hear, but that you know you need to hear. That's what this spread is for. The Harsh Truth spread serves as a blunt friend, but in a private space.

This spread is laid out in two lines, three cards on each line, with the "truth cards" at the center of each line. Truth is *central* in life, but especially in this spread.

Shuffle the deck and pull cards for this spread:

Card 1: *What you want to be true*

Card 2: *What you don't want to be true*

Card 3: *What is true*

Card 4: *What you want to happen*

Card 5: *What you don't want to happen*

Card 6: *What will happen*

*Now, reflect on what you pulled. Is there a connection between **Card 2** (your fears) and **Card 5**?*

_____

_____

_____

*How did you feel when you pulled **Card 3**?*

_____

_____

_____

Did you learn anything new?

_____

_____

_____

Has this helped you find closure with the hardship?

_____

_____

_____

Breakup Closure Tarot Spread

Breakups can be extremely difficult to heal from. It's not always because of the heartbreak, really. A lot of hurt in breakups come from mourning the person that you thought you would be. When you end a relationship, you're ending a future that you thought was yours. Tarot is a great tool for healing, and this exercise shows you how.

Pull cards for the tarot spread below. Write down your cards as you go.

1. *What happened?*

2. *What was right about this relationship?*

3. *What was wrong about it?* _____

4. *Why was breaking up necessary?* _____

5. *What will our relationship look like in the future?* _____

6. *What advice is there for the next relationship?* _____

Write down your findings. Does anything surprise you about your cards? Is there anything that doesn't make sense?

_____

_____

_____

_____

_____

_____

_____

_____

_____

_____

_____

_____

_____

_____

_____

_____

_____

_____

_____

Redefining "Negative" Cards

When we go through hardship, it can be difficult to think about the good side of things. This exercise doesn't necessarily focus on the situation you're going through. Instead, it's a practice for recognizing how healing can come from negative outcomes.

Go through the entire deck and choose all the deeply negative cards that you can find. Don't think about why you consider them to be negative. It could be their meanings, the sentiment they bring, or even the pictures on the card: It doesn't matter.

    Place them in front of you in an upright position. Draw (yes, draw) each of the cards in this the space below. This isn't an art project; the drawings can be basic. As you draw, recognize what symbols you're choosing to represent for each card. Consider how they symbolize your fears or dislikes.

Look at the cards all together. Write out a couple of adjectives that describe your feelings as you look at them:

_____

_____

_____

Now turn all the cards upside down. What looks different? How do the pictures make you feel in comparison to the upright positions? Draw them again with this new perspective:

Write a description of your feelings as you look at them:

_____

_____

_____

Loss + Reflection Tarot Spread

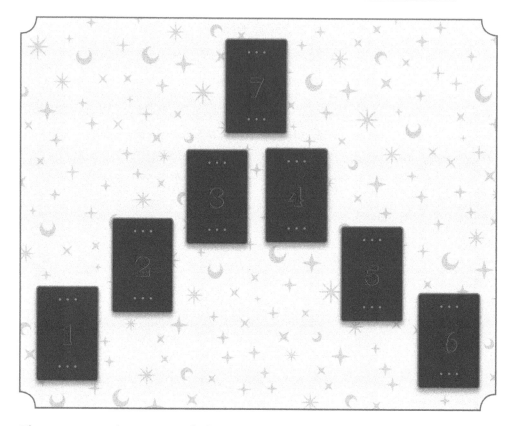

This tarot spread is meant to help you reflect on loss—whatever loss you've experienced—in a constructive and productive way.

First, let's pull a signifier card for your loss: _____

    Place this card at the top of the table in front of you. Meditate on it for a moment. Why do you think this particular card came up to signify your loss?

_____

_____

_____

_____

Now that you've covered what the loss is and what it means to you, let's move on to the tarot spread that will help you find reflection and purpose. Pull cards for the spread below:

1. _My mind's reaction to this loss_

2. _My heart's reaction_

3. _My body's reaction_

4. _My spirit's reaction_

5. _What needs the most TLC?_

6. _Have I found healing?_

7. _What did I learn from this loss?_

How are the first four cards similar or different from one another? For example, has your mind moved on before your heart? Have your mind, body, and heart moved on before your spirit has had time to learn the lesson? Reflect on the answers here.

The Fool's Journey

In the tarot deck, the Major Arcana is representative of the metaphorical cycles we all go through in life. We are constantly going through different chapters, experiencing ups and downs. That's just life. The Major Arcana represents one full chapter or life lesson, which is why we may experience a "Tower moment" more than once in our life. Life is full of lessons.

With regards to a hardship you are experiencing, this exercise asks you to locate where you fall in the Major Arcana. Are you at the thirteenth card, Death? Or are you further into the process at, let's say, the twentieth card, Judgment?

Lay out the full twenty-two-card Major Arcana section in front of you. From there, pick out the card that best represents how you're feeling. Are you at a spiritual awakening, like Judgment? Or are you still trying to find a sense of clarity and understanding, like The Hanged Man?

What card best represents how you feel about your hardship? _____

Circle the number of this Major Arcana card below:

1	2	3	4	5	6	7	8	9	10	11
12	13	14	15	16	17	18	19	20	21	22

Based on what you circled, you have an idea of how close you are to the end of this cycle.

Find the Lesson

It's often so hard to identify why something is happening and whether it can possibly be for the greater good. Some experiences, especially those arising from bigotry and oppression, don't feel like they offer much for us to take away as lessons or opportunities. But some hardships give us a chance to learn from and reassess our situations. This exercise uses reversals to help you look for some kind of meaning, or opportunities for progress, from your hardship.

First, pick three cards out of the tarot deck that you feel best identify with your difficult situation. It's likely, especially if the experience is quite recent, that the cards you choose reflect your pain. They can be upright or reversed, depending on how you're feeling.

These three cards represent the PROBLEM. Write them down here:

Card 1: _____

Card 2: _____

Card 3: _____

Now let's find the LESSON. Turn the cards upside down so the spread shows each card in a reversed position. What do you see now? How can each of the cards be interpreted as a lesson to learn?

Card 1: _____

Card 2: _____

Card 3: _____

Write a Gratitude Letter

One of the best ways to find healing from trauma or hardship is to express gratitude for all that you gained from the experience. It sounds funny, but it tends to work. Ultimately, not every experience can be met with gratitude, but this process can help you come to terms with an experience and release the power it has over you. In this exercise, we're going to write a "thank you" letter to a hardship.

First, pull three cards that express what we can be grateful for regarding this situation:

_____

_____

_____

Now go ahead and write out your letter. In each blank, write down the name of the designated card or what you associate with it.

Dear _____,

You made me feel pain, hurt, and loneliness. But I'm grateful for you because you helped me learn _____ [**Card 1**]. You also made me realize that I'm much happier when I'm not _____ [**Card 2**]. And finally, I'm grateful for this experience because _____ [**Card 3**].

Thank you for the growth.

Best,

_____

KEY TAKEAWAYS

Tarot is a wonderful tool for coming to terms with an obstacle in front of you, finding clarity or closure in a tough situation, and identifying growth opportunities that come from hard experiences.

It can be hard to step outside of ourselves when we are heavily tied to an emotional situation. In fact, it can be damned near impossible to find even one positive outlook depending on how deeply integrated you are with the obstacle. You can lean on tarot cards to help you identify not only emotions and areas of pain, but also points of growth and patterns that can help you move forward.

◆ Finding your personal sources of strength will support you during times of hardship.

◆ Tarot helps us discover insightful solutions and new perspectives on difficult times.

◆ Life has repeating cycles and chapters. Tarot draws our attention to these patterns and helps us determine where we fall in the time line.

◆ Tarot, as an outside perspective, can help you identify points of clarity, gratitude, and growth.

CHAPTER 10

MANIFESTING JOY AND RESILIENCE

To manifest is to bring thoughts into reality. Generally, we aim to manifest positive thoughts, but why is joy grouped with resilience in this chapter? Manifestation is a slow process and resilience is typically the key to getting through that process. Willpower and steadfast determination will get you through the tough times as you wait for your manifestations to come to life.

This section of the workbook uses tarot to explore different methods of manifestation, recognition (such as how to see current blessings), and tools for finding personal strength levels. Overall, this section will encourage you to dream big and help you feel prepared to manifest anything you desire in this life.

Small Manifestation How-To

This exercise takes a very hands-on approach to manifestation. This is an especially helpful activity for those who have never practiced manifestation before.

Manifestation is driven by our thoughts. We are constantly manifesting based on what we're thinking. If we're putting out more positive and grateful thoughts, we are naturally attracting more of the same in our life. Manifestation can be general, or it can be so detailed that you can attract very specific things into your life.

In this exercise, we'll use tarot as a way to manifest something completely random.

Find time in the morning for this exercise. Start by shuffling the cards. As you shuffle, ask the cards what you should manifest today. Whatever card flies out first will hold the answer.

Write it down here: _____

Looking at the card, what specific imagery do you see? For example, you may see a table. Perhaps you'll ask to manifest a small, square table as you see in the card.

Write down your intention for the day: _____

Return to this page at the end of the day and answer this question: Did you manifest your intention? Circle your answer.

YES   NO

Manifestation Card

Not sure what your life needs? This exercise will help you identify it. We can use the tarot deck to identify what is already close within your reach so you can focus on manifesting that.

As you shuffle the cards, ask them: What is missing in my life? What should I manifest?

Pull one card and write it down: _____

Next, write down what you believe this card represents: _____

That's your manifestation card. Keep it in a visible and handy place. Every time you see it, meditate on the intention. (That's visualization at its easiest.)

To add extra oomph to your manifestation process, write down three positive affirmations that you can repeat every time you see the card. Make sure that these affirmations are related to the overall intention. For example, if your intention is to manifest a six-figure career, then a positive affirmation might be "I am worthy of a six-figure job."

1. _____

2. _____

3. _____

Elemental Manifestation

The last two exercises may have given you some ideas for what intention you want to manifest, but now what? You might find you are a little stuck. What's next?

Rituals are an easy way to boost your manifesting energy, especially during potent moon phases like new or full moons. There are many different types of rituals, and they all use one or more of the four elements: earth, fire, water, and air.

With your intention in mind, shuffle the deck and pull a card that will tell you what kind of ritual to use. As you pick one, notice the suit. Which suit did you choose? Circle below.

PENTACLES   WANDS   SWORDS   CUPS

Next, use the table below to determine which element your suit matches up with:

PENTACLES	EARTH
WANDS	FIRE
SWORDS	AIR
CUPS	WATER

Here are a few quick suggestions for how to use your element in a ritual:

Earth. *Write down your intention and bury it in the ground alongside a seed.*

Fire. *Write down your intention and burn it while repeating affirmations.*

Air. *Write down your intention on a small piece of paper, shred it, and let it blow away in the wind.*

Water. *Repeat your affirmations while thinking of your intention as you make a cup of tea. Drink.*

Resilience Meter

Let's say you're going through a taxing time and you want to know how much energy you have left. This exercise is supposed to help you locate where you're at and help you identify whether you need to take a mental break.

Separate the Major Arcana from the Minor Arcana in the deck. We're going to use the Major Arcana section. Shuffle the cards and ask the deck where your resilience is at.

Pull one card or note if a flier card comes into play. Write down the name of the card: _____

Note the number of the Major Arcana. Use The Fool (0) as a representation of the highest amount of resilience. Use The World (XXI) as an indicator of very low resilience (i.e., in need of a mental break).

Circle the number of the Major Arcana card:

0	1	2	3	4	5	6	7	8	9	10	11
12	13	14	15	16	17	18	19	20	21		

Based on your resilience card, do you need a mental break? Circle one.

YES   NO

Color-Me-Happy

This fun exercise focuses on The Sun card, the most optimistic, bright, and visionary card in the deck. Coloring in tarot cards allows us to soak in all of the card's energy and can help us focus on the small details we may have previously missed.

Color in The Sun card on the next page however you see fit.

When you finish, reflect on how you felt as you colored in the lines. Did it bring joy? Happiness? Positivity?

THE SUN

Joy Tarot Spread

Do you need a pick-me-up? Is it time to give yourself a little love and find joy again? This tarot spread serves as the energy boost you need to keep on trekking toward your goals.

Shuffle your cards and pull this spread:

Card 1: *Where are my joy levels?*

Card 2: *How am I blocking or resisting joy in my life?*

Card 3: *Why am I doing this?*

Card 4: *What is a way to "unblock" myself from reaching happiness?*

Card 5: *What is something that makes me incredibly happy?*

Card 6: *Who is someone that makes me incredibly happy?*

Card 7: *What advice can you give me?*

Reflect on the cards using the following prompts. Circle your answers.

My joy levels:

BAD   OKAY   HAPPY

Are you blocking joy?

YES   NO

Do you have someone who makes you very happy?

YES   NO

What suit appeared for **Card 5**? *This should help you identify the type of activity you need.*

PENTACLES   WANDS   SWORDS   CUPS

Do **Card 4** *and* **Card 7** *have anything in common?*

YES   NO

If so, what do they have in common?

_____

_____

_____

_____

What Blessings Are Coming?

Hard times are inevitable. When we feel low or defeated, it's important to intentionally focus on the good things in life, as well as the good things still to come. Thankfully, tarot enables us to identify some of these blessings that have yet to appear.

Use this exercise to keep you motivated as you wait for your manifestations to come to life or as you look ahead toward a brand-new chapter in your life.

Shuffle your tarot deck. This exercise will use flier cards (cards that fly out of the deck, not ones that you pull for yourself).

Ask the cards: What blessings are on their way to me?

Shuffle intently until two or three cards fall out of the deck. Write them down:

_____

_____

_____

_____

Reflect on what the cards mean to you. What do they represent? What are they bringing? Notice the suit associated with each card, as this can indicate the area of life affected. Also note whether court cards appear, as this can suggest people coming into your life. Finally, take particular note of Aces; they represent new beginnings.

_____

_____

_____

_____

_____

Happy Song

Music is a natural catalyst for emotion. When the right song plays, a memory, a feeling, or even a sense of renewed energy can flow through you. This exercise aims to harness the power of music to channel joy. Let's find your happy song.

_____

Go through your music library. If you have a favorite playlist, start there. Play ten seconds of each song to give them a test run. Note how you feel during these ten seconds. Are you peaceful? Calm? Excited? Happy? We want the happy song.

Once you've found your song, write it down: _____

Next, play your song. During the first half, feel the excitement and the joy. Listen to the rhythm, flow to the beat, and allow natural emotion to take over.

After the first half, once you're full of emotions, shuffle your cards and wait for a flier card to pop out. Whichever card comes up is directly linked to your most incandescent happiness.

Write the name of that card: _____

How does your song relate to your card? Does it feel similar to you? When you look at your card, do you hear your song?

_____

_____

_____

_____

_____

_____

_____

_____

_____

Willpower Tarot Spread

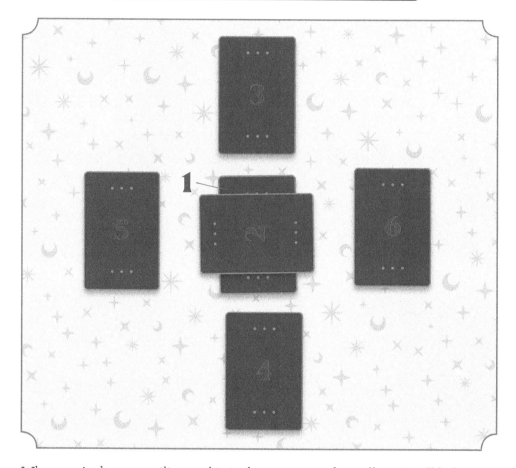

When you're low on resilience, this is the tarot spread to call on. It will help you through even the slowest or lowest of times. This exercise keeps you pushing toward your goals so you're able to find joy.

The spread layout places a signifier card that represents you at the center of the "power cards." These four cards surrounding "you" signify sources where you can draw your power from. Additionally, one card crosses the signifier card as a representation of what blocks you. You'll be able to see what blocks you as well as what you can draw on to remove the block.

Shuffle the cards and ask them for personal strength. Pull for the spread below:

Card 1: *Me (signifier)*

Card 2: *The blockage*

Card 3: *My strengths*

Card 4: *My skills*

Card 5: *My wisdom*

Card 6: *My potential*

As you draw your cards, reflect on the answers. Write down the insights that surprise you the most:

_____

_____

_____

_____

_____

_____

*Using **Card 4** and **Card 6** as guides, will you be able to draw out more willpower? Circle one.*

YES   NO

KEY TAKEAWAYS

Tarot cards can be used to manifest your thoughts, goals, and dreams, as well as help you foster resilience as you work on manifestation. The first few exercises in this chapter demonstrate what manifestation is and how it works. The exercises in the middle of the chapter promote tapping into more joy. The final exercises focus on potential and opportunities ahead.

With a proper introduction to manifestation, anything is possible, especially when using tarot. Dream big and use the cards to help you manifest everything you desire in life. Remember that manifestation can be a slow process, so it is crucial to foster your resilience and create joy along the way.

◆ Manifestation is the realization of positive thoughts and intentions.

◆ Tarot enables us to identify blessings that are coming our way, helping us on the road toward manifesting our goals.

◆ Manifestation can be used to attract something very specific or something more general.

◆ Tarot can help you identify rituals to tap into and boost your manifesting energy on a regular basis.

◆ With resilience and the right mindset, you can manifest anything you desire.

A Final Note

If nothing else, I hope the exercises in this workbook proved that tarot cards are more than just a fun party trick used to tell fortunes. These cards can act as a powerful tool for deep reflection and self-analysis. As a self-help tool, tarot can reveal extremely in-depth insights into who we are. Like a therapist, the cards are an unbiased entity that can help us identify our pitfalls, where triggers stem from, and how the past affects the present.

The reason? Tarot provides a safe space for vulnerability. Tarot cards are a third-party outlet—without feelings, ambiguity, or consciousness—so they can more easily send direct, logical messages to you. There is a healthy amount of distance between you and what they have to say, because the cards are not concerned with external pressures or forces. In fact, sometimes it's easier to listen to a deck of cards than a real person. You can't fight with an inanimate object if you don't like the answer.

Keep in mind that the tarot deck itself is not the one in charge. *You* give tarot its powers. Tarot works off the energy of the person who is holding it, so you are the source of intuition, not tarot.

As you work through and revisit the exercises in this workbook, I hope they provide you with a new perspective on tarot. But more importantly, I hope this process shows you just how intuitive, strong, and powerful you are as an individual. I hope the exercises help you build the confidence you need to gather information. Finally, I hope they shed light on who you are now, who you want to be, and how to get where you want to go.

As you continue your journey, remember that tarot is a free-flowing practice. You don't need a workbook to do these exercises. You can modify the activities to suit your needs or be inspired to create your own exercises and spreads. The methods are flexible: do what works for you, pick decks that speak to you, mold the card meanings in whatever way you see fit. Tarot reading is a balance between what is taught and what is felt. As you locate that middle ground and home in on your intuition, you'll find that self-healing and self-analysis come faster and easier.

Resources

APPS

Golden Thread Tarot (GoldenThreadTarot.com):

Learn the cards with this user-friendly app. Based on the Golden Thread tarot deck, this app offers tarot meanings as well as lessons on how to read the cards.

Labyrinthos Academy app (App.Labyrinthos.co):

Learn tarot card meanings on the go using your mobile device. Labyrinthos doesn't just have a stellar website; they also offer an app that helps you learn tarot meanings.

BOOKS

Holistic Tarot: An Integrative Approach to Using Tarot for Personal Growth, by Benebell Wen

This book is thick and informative, and explores each tarot card with an in-depth perspective. This book is ideal for those who have an analytic approach to learning.

Mary K. Greer's 21 Ways to Read a Tarot Card, by Mary K. Greer

This book shows how in depth tarot can really get. There are more ways to read a tarot card than just upright and reversed. This book aims to help you uncover just how many perspectives you can use to approach the cards.

365 Tarot Spreads: Revealing the Magic in Each Day, by Sasha Graham

This book provides one tarot spread a day. There are infinite ways to create a spread, and this book can inspire you to find new ways to work with tarot and tarot spreads.

PODCASTS

Awakened Tarot by Jaclyn Kitzman

This podcast provides in-depth discussions on just one card per episode. It brings to light new ways to view each card so you're able to make your own interpretations.

Tarot Bytes by Theresa Reed

This podcast is run by renowned tarot reader Theresa Reed. Her episodes are typically thirty minutes or less, so they are great to listen to during your morning commute.

WEBSITES

Biddy Tarot (biddytarot.com):

If you're still learning the card meanings, this website is, hands down, the best place to get your information. I especially recommend it because of the way the author incorporates more traditional meanings into her practice.

Labyrinthos Academy (labyrinthos.co):

This is another great website that offers free information on tarot spreads, exercises, and tarot card meanings. The meanings found here represent a more developed and modern take on tarot cards.

References

Esselmont, Brigit. "Learn the Tarot Card Meanings." Biddy Tarot, May 12, 2022. biddytarot.com/tarot-card-meanings.

Fisher, Kate. "7 Tarot Activities to Do on a Rainy (or Quarantined) Day!" Daily Tarot Girl, March 17, 2020. daily-tarot-girl.com/2020/03/16/7-tarot-activities -to-do-on-a-rainy-or-quarantined-day.

Gaudet, Christiana. "Finding the Theme: A Tarot Exercise." Christiana Gaudet, Tarot Grandmaster, February 13, 2020. christianagaudet.com/ personal-blog/2020/2/12/finding-the-theme-a-tarot-exercise.

Gong, Tina. "Tarot Card Meanings List: 78 Cards by Suit, Element, and Zodiac." Labyrinthos Academy. Accessed July 14, 2022. labyrinthos.co/blogs/ tarot-card-meanings-list.

Graham, Sasha. *365 Tarot Spreads: Revealing the Magic in Each Day.* Woodbury, MN: Llewellyn Publications, 2014.

Greer, Mary K. *Mary K. Greer's 21 Ways to Read a Tarot Card.* Woodbury, MN: Llewellyn Publications, 2008.

Kitzman, Jacyln. Produced by Jacyln Kitzman. *Awakened Tarot*, 2020–2022. anchor.fm/awakenedtarot.

"Little Red Tarot: Indie Tarot & Radical Magic." Little Red Tarot. Accessed July 14, 2022. littleredtarot.com.

Reed, Theresa. Produced by Theresa Reed, The Tarot Lady. *Tarot Bytes*, 2016–2022. thetarotlady.com/tarot-bytes.

Wen, Benebell. *Holistic Tarot: An Integrative Approach to Using Tarot for Personal Growth.* Berkeley, CA: North Atlantic Books, 2015.

Index

Acknowledgments

I would like to thank my tarot community and support system for making tarot an accessible and acceptable tool for self-help and personal development. You all have truly changed my life.

About the Author

Maisy Bristol is a tarot reader and astrologer who guides individuals toward clarity and self-development. Specializing in relationships, trauma healing, mental health, and life choices, her readings encourage clients to dial into their own inner wisdom and view life changes with a positive outlook. In addition to tarot readings, astrological readings, and tarot courses, Maisy offers a personalized tarot and astrology subscription service, Tarotpy, that helps clients accomplish their personal growth goals. Maisy's work has been featured in Bustle, Well + Good, MindBodyGreen, Refinery29, and POPSUGAR, among other publications. She lives happily in Montana with her horses, dogs, and chickens.

CPSIA information can be obtained
at www.ICGtesting.com
Printed in the USA
JSHW031746211122
33587JS00006B/51